"Along with an entrepreneur class in high school, *Think Like an Entrepreneur* should be required reading. So many people choose a career based on making other people happy only to find that years down the road they are miserable. Imagine what the world would be like if everyone had the courage to begin their career following their dreams."

—Julie Barnes, Writer, aspiring artist and author of
So You Want to Start a Business…Now What?

"*Think Like an Entrepreneur* took my current thinking outside of the box. Whether you are an Entrepreneur or taking the steps to be one, Deborah takes your vision of confidence, creativity, motivation and inspiration to the next level."

—Susan Vernicek, Founder and Owner of *Identity* Magazine

"*Think Like an Entrepreneur* just nails it! Deb has done what most don't want to do. She tells us the truth about being in business for yourself. Through her personal accounts of her journey from the land of Corporate America to entrepreneurship she shares what it REALLY takes to be in business for yourself. This book shows you how becoming an entrepreneur goes way beyond just having a business plan. I would definitely add this book to your required reading list!"

—Annemarie Segaric, author of *Step into the Right Career*

THINK LIKE AN ENTREPRENEUR

TRANSFORMING YOUR CAREER AND TAKING CHARGE OF YOUR LIFE

80 CR

Published by Bright Street Books™
Piscataway, NJ
877-426-6107

ISBN: 978-0-9842926-0-8

DEDICATION

This book is dedicated to my mom, Ruth D. Bailey, who believed in my dream even when I had doubts. I owe it all to you.

CONTENTS

INTRODUCTION

When I graduated from high school, I wanted to go into business for myself. I didn't though, because I had no idea where to begin. No one I knew had their own business. Everyone I knew worked for someone else. They planned for retirement and receiving their pensions. At the time I thought that life was finding some sort of career, working very hard for years, then hopefully retiring at 65 and finally doing what I wanted. That was life. But I didn't accept that this was the kind of life I wanted to live. Deep down I felt myself rebelling against this life sentence of drudgery. That's how I saw it.

You see, I've been a writer for as long as I can remember. I'm a creative person who is in my element when I'm creating something. Doing busy work or punching a clock is for me, like dying. I've always believed that life is too precious, too wonderful to throw away on working for money. Let me explain myself. Money is certainly necessary to having a comfortable life. My problem is that I could never accept that I should make money the ends instead of the means. I also couldn't accept that I should work at a job that I didn't love just for the money.

That was my view when I was younger, and you may well say that it's a naïve view. I disagree. Many of us have been convinced that work shouldn't be enjoyed, but tolerated. So, we accept the bad treatment, the frustration and the lack of fulfillment because we've come to believe it's normal. I say it's not. The norm is to live a live of fulfillment and achievement of your goals and desires. Why wait until some catastrophic event happens and then suddenly you realize what you've been missing? Why not realize it right now?

Before I went into the corporate world I was quite happy in my job. I picked an industry that I wanted to work in, and took the steps to enter it. But eventually once I worked in the corporate environment I found that it didn't suit me at all. I strained against the restrictions and the rules put in place, it seemed, to keep people operating within the most narrow of scopes. I hated punching a clock and I hated having no control over my own environment. Worst of all, I disliked that my job never utilized my skills and my intelligence.

I found myself in situations where the less capable you were the more likely you would be in authority. People would gripe and complain and engage in petty activities like gossiping about each other or others who they found intimidating. There were times that I also engaged in this negativity. Why? Because I was caught up in the frustration of being in an environment that choked off creativity and kept people in a loop of conformity, fear and a real lack of purpose. I worked very hard so that I would not have time to think about how unfulfilled I was. I stayed in motion in an effort to never have enough time to look around and see what I'd created for myself.

During my years in corporate I stopped writing. Once I started writing again, I considered leaving my career and going back to a creative career. It took me many years before I actually took that step, but once I did I wondered why I'd waited so long. I'm still in the process of recovering that creative part of myself.

It has not been an easy process. I'm not changing into a new person, but recovering parts of myself that are already there. That is probably true of most people. Over the years we've buried the parts of us that were the most reflective of who we really are. In order to go along to get along, we've let other stuff pile up like scar tissue covering over a wound. In order to uncover what's underneath all that; we have to pull it off again. Sounds like a painful process, doesn't it? It some ways it is, and in other ways it's liberating. It all depends on your point of view.

I left the corporate world and entered entrepreneurship because I never wanted to be controlled by a workplace ever again. Like a lot of people I've had my share of obnoxious managers and negative work environments. I've struggled against office politics, bigoted mindsets, and Borg-like "resistance is futile" company cultures. All through those experiences I kept one idea in mind: that life does not have to be this way. Life is beautiful and fun and an adventure—or at least it should be. That belief is what I carried with me when I left full-time employment behind.

As a contractor I found freedom in being able to do my work without being involved in the politics. I enjoyed the experience and started my business as a virtual assistant on the side. Why a virtual assistant? Because I was afraid to be a writer. I figured that I still couldn't completely go back to being creative, so I hedged my bets by offering administrative support with writing thrown in.

Ultimately I decided to call myself a writer and drop the VA part of my business. Once I did that I got business, though not a lot. Part of the reason for that could have been because I'd been told by other writers how I shouldn't set my sights too high. I should just settle for less of an income and my status as a new member of the starving artist set. It was funny even though I left the corporate world I didn't leave limiting beliefs behind. This goes to show you that your situation has less to do with the environment and more to do with a person's state of mind. If they expect limits they will get them.

It was easy for me to embrace this new set of limits since I hadn't released the ones I was still carrying around. It was like changing one pair of shoes for another. I simply slipped out of my corporate shoes and stepped into my entrepreneur shoes without ever changing anything else.

What I discovered was that you can't just step from one into the other and have a successful transition. Often the transition is not the actual change from A to B; it's what happens after you're doing B. More than likely you're still operating as though you're doing A. If A and B are the same, no problem. But if you're going from corporate employee to entrepreneur, it's sort of the same as going from the earth to the moon. If you're not prepared for the new environment you will not survive.

This is what no one ever talks about when discuss starting a business. They talk about business plans and marketing plans and everything in between. What they never mention is the plan for transitioning from a corporate job to your own business. They don't mention the mental and emotional changes that you go through during the transition. Perhaps its because the people who write business books have never been in the rank and file. If they were in the corporate world they were executives or consultants. Or perhaps they're from academia or have never been a corporate employee for any significant length of time. No one talks about what happens when you've been brought up to believe in "work hard and get a pension" and suddenly that all goes away. What happens when your 401K is empty, you have no subsidized health insurance and your retirement plan consists of an I.O.U.?

My entire life was structured around the concepts I'd seen my family go through and what I'd been raised to believe. A life of hard work (whether you liked it or not was optional) and a (hopefully) healthy senior citizen retirement. In the meantime, you contribute to your 401K, keep your head down and stay employed. What happens when you're responsible for generating your own income? How does it feel when as a business owner you may have a nice title, such as CEO or President, in addition to a title such as custodian, administrative assistant and receptionist. Suddenly titles and income don't have the same connotations as they did when you were employed by someone else. If you define yourself by your income, or what you can purchase, you may find yourself disappointed with this new way of life. Now you have to define yourself by your accomplishments, and you might be the only one who knows what they are for a while.

It's a completely different world than the one you may have been used to in a structured corporate environment. You have to believe in yourself a whole lot because there's no manager giving you an appraisal and telling you if you're doing it right. You have to learn to live outside of a structure that gives you the illusion of life-long security. There is no security in being an entrepreneur and there are no guarantees.

I've encountered people who have made the transition and are still trapped in their corporate personas. Either they're resentful because they have to sacrifice the trappings of security or they are reluctant to make any investment, believing they can build a business with as little effort as possible. But you can't make a transition and remain unchanged. It's impossible.

When I became an entrepreneur I was looking for freedom. I didn't do it necessarily to have a business, but I wanted to be responsible for generating my own income. I had no idea how to run a business, and I made many mistakes along the way, but I couldn't bear the thought of returning to a corporate life. What I found was that being an entrepreneur is very similar to being a creative person. You use creativity, intuition and you take risks. Most importantly you take action because if you don't nothing will get done. These are qualities that some people have naturally and others have to learn. They are traits that help you to not just survive, but thrive no matter what's going on in the world around you.

There's an added benefit to using these qualities. You will open the door to the parts of yourself that you may have hidden and forgotten about. Once you open that up there's no going back. You can't pretend that you didn't know what you really desired. Walk through that door and you will never be the same person again.

HOW TO USE THIS BOOK

In this book you'll discover how small shifts in thinking can help you connect with your power and your passion. Transformation begins when you see how to remove the blocks to living a fulfilling and purposeful life.

In learning to navigate this new world (and new life) I discovered that there are entrepreneurial characteristics that are essential to surviving and thriving. What I also found is that these traits—which I also call "success traits"—can be adapted by non-entrepreneurs as well.

Each chapter will give you a step along the journey to move from the employee to the entrepreneurial mindset. You'll also find motivational "coaching tips" that include questions for you to answer in this book or your journal. Take it step by step and allow yourself to work through each stage at your own pace.

In the For More Information section you'll find a selection of motivational books and videos that can inspire you and will hopefully entertain you as well. Staying focused on your vision doesn't mean you can't take time to relax and to laugh, so be sure you regularly take the opportunity to do both.

I wish you joy as you learn how to shift your thinking and make powerful changes in your life!

"Reach high, for stars lie hidden in your soul.
Dream deep, for every dream precedes the goal."
—Pamela Vaull Starr

CHAPTER 1: GETTING STARTED

"Within you right now is the power to do things you never dreamed possible. This power becomes available to you just as soon as you can change your beliefs."

–Dr. Maxwell Maltz

You might be wondering why entrepreneurial thinking is so important. Is it something you can apply to your life even if you don't have a business? The answer is yes!

So, What Exactly is Entrepreneurial Thinking?

Entrepreneurs are responsible for creating their own incomes and so they have to be open to finding creative solutions. Entrepreneurs must always be evolving and growing so that they can be ahead of the curve, not behind it. They have to see opportunities where other people may not see anything, in addition to possessing a great deal of creativity and a large tolerance for risk. In an environment where there is a great deal of churn in the economy, people who can stay focused in the face of uncertainty are the ones who will be able to prosper. Those who are only focused on losses and are paralyzed by fear will have a difficult time making it through. This is why having an entrepreneurial mindset is perfect for the global financial shifts that we've all been experiencing.

For instance, using entrepreneurial thinking can help you when:

- You've experienced a job loss

- You want to change careers and don't know how to transfer your current skills

- You want to start a business

- You want to get "unstuck" and move towards your goals

- You want to manage uncertainty due to life changes and transitions

- You want to find your purpose

- You want to be open to new opportunities personally and professionally

Why would a non-entrepreneur want to adopt an entrepreneurial mindset?
No one wants to feel that his or her work has no purpose. It's hard to get through a day or feel any enthusiasm for your work if you feel that none of it matters. One reason why people go into business for themselves is because they want more freedom over their lives. They don't want to be in an environment where they spend the day reacting to the decisions of others.

If you're ready to adopt entrepreneurial behaviors such as taking more risks and creating a vision for what you want to achieve, you'll be less likely to get stuck in a career rut. It means taking responsibility for your decisions and for the results.

Here are tips to get into an entrepreneurial mindset in your career right now:

1. Take an honest look at your work situation. How do things look in your company and in your industry? Are there growth opportunities?

2. Be open to learning and growing. If your skills have not been updated in years, find opportunities to upgrade them now.

3. What's your vision for your future? Where do you see yourself in six months or in a year? Are you willing to take steps to reach your goal?

4. Become more of a risk taker. Is there a project that you'd like to work on or a new process you'd like to introduce to your department? Are you willing to share your ideas or make a request for what you want?

Learn to trust yourself. If you don't have confidence in yourself or your ideas, it will be difficult for you to take charge of your career. You have to believe that you deserve to have a better experience and that you do have something to offer.

"SUCCESS TRAITS"

Although there are a lot of qualities that a successful entrepreneur may possess, the ones that non-entrepreneurs can adopt relatively quickly are listed below. As I've mentioned, these characteristics aren't only for the entrepreneurs, they can be used by anyone who wants to find more success and fulfillment. Let's take a look at each one:

Creating a Vision

- What do you really want?

- Where do you see yourself?

- Picture yourself in your ideal situation

Connecting with your Creativity

- Think outside of the box

- Don't make future decisions based on past experiences

- Be open to new approaches

Trusting your Intuition

- What do you feel is right for you?

- Listen to your "inner voice" when making decisions

- Trust that you know what's best for you

Taking Action

- Make a decision once you have the information that you need

- Be proactive instead of being a victim of circumstances

- Not making a decision is also a decision!

Applying the traits

You may wonder how these traits come into play in everyday life. Let's look at some examples of why they're important, and how they can be applied.

Entrepreneurs must use creativity when...

- They are looking for new sources of funding

- They want to create a new product or service

- They are brainstorming ideas

Entrepreneurs need a vision so they can...

- Stay focused on their goals

- Stay motivated even when they don't see the result of their work

- See the outcome so they can "be" it before they "see" it

Entrepreneurs need to trust their intuition so that...

- They can believe in themselves

- They can get inner direction on what steps to take

- They can rely on their own judgment when it comes to decision making

Entrepreneurs have to take action because...

- If they don't take action nothing will happen

- They'll be bombarded with ideas that never come into being

- They're easily distracted and will not follow through on what they started

Now you can see why I call these "entrepreneur success traits!" Without these traits it will be hard for anyone to reach his or her goals and experience success and fulfillment.

"What else are we going to live by if not dreams?"

–Jill Robinson

CHAPTER 2: VISION

*"The future belongs to those who believe
in the beauty of their dreams."*
—Eleanor Roosevelt

Don't confuse having a vision with having daydreams—though one can lead to the other. If you spend a lot of time picturing yourself in a new career or living in a different place, then those daydreams can point you in the direction of your vision.

Too often daydreams are dismissed as time wasters because we tend to under-value dreams in general. However once you start to see those images and allow yourself to feel good about what you are seeing, you are now connecting with your vision. An extremely important component of these images is your feelings about them. Those feelings are what will propel you forward and help you to manifest your vision into reality. Just as athletes picture themselves performing their sports before they actually do them, you must also picture yourself living your vision—and you must experience the feelings associated with that vision.

You may find that once you connect with your vision that it is uncomfortable for you to accept that it can be yours. I've had this experience a few times. I wanted something so bad, then I created the vision for it and felt the feelings of achieving it. But the feelings of achievement were intimidating and I backed off. It's hard to imagine backing off from something you say you want, but that happens all too often. Perhaps it seems to big for us to achieve or we're afraid to claim it for our own.

If you've spent a lifetime being told that you'll never get what you want and to put your desires last (or forget them entirely) it won't be easy to accept that your vision can become real. Sometimes we back off because we don't want to give up our anxieties and fears. If we've told ourselves a story that says we will always be defeated by life, then it's going to be hard to step into the role of victor. If this vision goes against our own beliefs, then we'll simply release the vision. That's why it is important to do the inner work first so that we can clear the way for the vision to become real.

You should also write down your thoughts and feelings about achieving this goal. Even if you don't regularly journal, it's okay. Don't let that stop you writing your ideas down. Keep a book or small notebook that you can carry with you wherever you go. Not only can it be used for your vision, but for your ideas and feelings about things in general. You'll be surprised at how much you can accomplish when you start writing things down!

If you don't have a clear picture of what you want to accomplish it will become all too easy to become distracted and lose your way. Without a vision you can end up running from one thing to another, trying to be all things to everyone. You can lose sight of what you really desire, which can ultimately lead you to ultimately giving up.

Getting Started

Begin by using your imagination. Involve all of your senses! Allow yourself to fully step into the experience. See it, feel it, be in it. Write about it! Create a vision board and place it where you can see it daily.

Having a vision will help get you through the down times. Your vision, your passion and your purpose will be like fuel propelling you forward in your journey.

Use this Process to Connect with your Purpose

You may not know what your purpose is at this moment, but if you're honest with yourself it will probably be tied very closely to your vision. Often we have no idea what we really want because we've made so many compromises along the way. Or perhaps you've always put your needs last, and don't feel comfortable making yourself the priority. Have fun with the vision process and you may find that what you picture in your mind is leading you to your purpose and to greater fulfillment in your life.

Steps to Holding Your Vision

Be willing to believe that you can have a different type of life, instead of repeating what's happened in the past.

- Practice "positive self-talk."

- Keep a journal and write down your ideas and goals.

"Your work is to discover your world, and then with all your heart give yourself to it."

–Buddha

GREAT EXPECTATIONS

"Now, I return to this young fellow. And
the communication I have got to make
is, that he has great expectations."

–Charles Dickens, "Great Expectations"

"Uncertainty and expectation are the joys of life.
Security is an insipid thing, and the
overtaking and possessing of a wish
discovers the folly of the chase."

–William Congreve, "Love for Love"

What happens when your desire for a different kind of life is in conflict with your current reality? We've been conditioned to believe that change has to occur on the outside first. This is what leads many people to believe that losing weight, or having the perfect relationship, perfect job or lots of money in the bank will solve all of their problems. It would be nice if it was true, but it's not. For some of you reading this, that's not exactly new information. For others, you may feel I'm only saying what coaches are supposed to say.

Speaking from my own experience, I know how difficult it can be to continue to believe in your dreams. The situation you're in can make those dreams seem totally ridiculous. That's when my inner critic decides to make an appearance and remind me of a few things. Real life is tough, you've got to try and survive and forget about fantasies. There have been times when I refused to believe I could have a better experience. Of course if you aren't getting what you want out of life, it is much more interesting to picture yourself as a brave survivor than someone who made bad choices.

So, if I'm honest with myself, I have to accept past decisions and learn from them. Then I have to open up the possibility that what happens next will not be a repeat of what has happened in the past. Easier said than done, but it is at the very heart of shifting your paradigm. It takes courage to see a thriving business when right now all you see are financial losses. Or see a healthy body where now there's one that's out of shape or unhealthy. It requires courage to open yourself up to loving again when you've been hurt or betrayed. It takes courage to take risks when you don't see how it will all turn out, or when people are telling you that you're crazy. It especially takes courage when someone tells you that they believe in you... that you can do it...but all you feel is fear.

It does sound like a cliché when you're told to move through the fear. However, that's the only way to get to the things we desire. I don't know exactly how it's all going to happen, but that's not really important. What is important is to believe that you can manifest your desires in spite of what you see around you in this moment.

When you're holding the vision for what you want—and you make the decision to move forward—you've got great expectations.

Questions to think about…

- What dreams have you put aside?

- Has fear been in the way of your creating a new life?

✎ to journal: **What is your "inner critic" saying to you right now?**

DREAMS

> *"Go confidently in the direction of your dreams. Live the life you've imagined."*
>
> –Henry David Thoreau

What are your big dreams?

Without action, dreams will never become reality. Are you taking steps towards achieving them? Or are they just dreams?

If you have a big dream that keeps getting put off, ask yourself why aren't you pursuing it? Does it seem too big or too unattainable? Have you been told that it's out of your reach?

Only you can decide if pursuing your dreams is worth the effort required to make them real. Are you ready to begin today?

ℂℂ

Questions to think about…

- How often do you let yourself dream?

- Have you taken any action to bring your dreams into reality?

to journal: **What do you see yourself achieving in the coming year?**

LIVING OUT LOUD

"Be brave enough to live life creatively. The creative is the place where no one else has ever been. You have to leave the city of your comfort and go into the wilderness of your intuition. You can't get there by bus, only by hard work and risk and by not quite knowing what you're doing. What you'll discover will be wonderful. What you'll discover will be yourself."

—Alan Alda

Have you ever shared an idea or a plan with someone, only to have them tell you that it wouldn't work? Or maybe you were told that you were crazy or had no common sense.

I've had that experience many times over the years, usually when I've mentioned my writing. I'll usually hear things such as: "books don't make any money" or "writers don't make any money" or "you'll never be as successful as..." Fill in a famous writer's name.

It's funny how writing can elicit such a weird response. When I mention my photography no one says, "you won't make money taking pictures!" I think there are two reasons for this. It could be because the feedback is reflecting my own fears of being a writer. Or it could be that the people giving the feedback have compromised and set aside their own dreams.

When you have a strong desire for something the next step is to create a vision for what you want. You have to see it and want it so much that there is no settling for something less. You'll also be less likely to be sidetracked by "well meaning" people who will share their opinion (whether you ask for it or not). When we're not really sure what we want we can end up conflicted and frustrated. Any opinion will seem better than our own, and we'll be locked in an internal struggle between what we desire and what we think we should do.

While all this is going on, our dreams will fade into the background as we accept limitations and focus on more "practical" avenues.

Are you prepared to look back on a life of compromise and "what might have been?" Do want to live with the regret that accompanies missed chances? Stop listening to people who feel it's their duty to tell you what you can't do. As the Nike slogan says, just do it.

It's time to stop hiding in the shadows. It's time to live out loud.

⟡ ⟢

Questions to think about…

- Have you ever received negative feedback when you've told someone about your aspirations?

- Have you considered hiring a coach or finding a mentor to provide you with support and accountability?

✎ to journal: **How often have you been stopped when you've hit roadblocks or resistance to your plans?**

CHAPTER 3: INTUITION

"Our deepest wishes are whispers of our authentic selves. We must learn to respect them. We must learn to listen."

—Sarah Ban Breathnach

An important part of being an entrepreneur is knowing when to listen to your "gut" feeling, your intuition. When I left the corporate world I received a great deal of good advice and a great deal of not-so-good advice. Unfortunately at the time I didn't know enough to be able to tell the difference. I never thought to look within and go with my feelings. Instead I went against them and didn't trust myself.

Learning to Trust Your Feelings

Have you ever been in a situation where you made a decision that didn't turn out well, then when you looked back you could see the warning signs? We've all had those experiences. As we were having the experience, we couldn't see the pitfalls. It wasn't until afterwards that we could understand where we went off track.

The catch is that usually we have to experience discomfort in order to be pushed to a higher level of understanding. As long as things are comfortable, we won't do very much to change the situation. Why should we? It's the discomfort that leads us to look for opportunities for change. Though in some cases we may get stuck hoping that things will change without our efforts, it's not very likely that will happen. Even if we don't make a decision about which action to take, that in itself is a decision! By not deciding we are deciding to go along with things as they are.

Once we find ourselves in an uncomfortable place, it becomes extremely important for us to trust our own judgment. Often we can go in circles, asking anyone and everyone for their advice. You know what happens then? We get so many different opinions that we become paralyzed and stay stuck.

There's nothing wrong with having a mentor or other person who you can trust to give you good advice. However, in the end only we know what's best for us. That's where trusting our intuition becomes most important and the key to our success. When we listen to ourselves we can maintain focus on our goals and our vision for what we want.

Trusting yourself can be a very tough if you're not used to doing it. There will be times where you're the only one who can see your vision. You won't get support and you may even be ridiculed. In those times it is so important to be able to see and feel what others can't.

Steps to Connecting With Your Intuition

Get into a habit of having quiet time so you can listen to your inner voice

Pay attention to your feelings. If you're feeling good about a decision it's probably in line with your desires. If you feel apprehension, there's a reason for it.

In addition to intuition, there has to be trust. If you don't trust your own perceptions you certainly won't trust "gut" feelings. Give yourself time to get used to this new behavior; there will be some trial and error involved!

It's very important to become aware of your feelings because they will be an indicator of what's best for you. It may be uncomfortable at first because you may not be used to trusting what you feel.

Unfortunately there are people who will waste no time in telling you that you're wrong or that they know what's best for you. If you trust them more than you trust yourself, then you won't believe in your own responses. Instead you'll dismiss them or accuse yourself of being "too sensitive" or misjudging the situation. Wrong! You know best what is right for you. Don't let yourself be taken off course by what others tell you what you should believe.

You may also have to get used to feeling a bit vulnerable during this process. It will be difficult to connect with your intuition if you're closed off. Often we can "turn off" our emotions in an effort to protect ourselves from being hurt. Unfortunately we're also preventing ourselves from having any real experience. Relying on logic and dismissing feelings as a sign of weakness will lead you to miss out on your own personal guidance system.

Release Control

When you release expectations over the outcome, you can be open to receiving guidance. You won't have preconceived ideas of what you believe should happen.

Instead you'll be open to taking a different road to where you want to be. Our perceptions are based on past experiences, so if we base new experiences on old ones we will stay stuck. We'll keep repeating past patterns over and over. In order to reach your vision for a new life experience, you'll have to accept that you don't know how events will unfold—you just have to be sure that they will lead you to the fulfillment of your dream.

The old stories we tell ourselves about what we're capable of will keep us in those same stories. How can you have a different life if you're holding on to old beliefs? If you've been told that you aren't smart enough or that you are too old—or too young—to accomplish your goals you won't take action. Those old stories will keep you limited and will ensure you are stuck in a loop of the same experiences.

For most of my life I've been told that writers don't make any money. The funny thing is it's usually people who have never written anything who have this belief! Unfortunately they've felt the need to share their limited views with me. Always be careful of people who can't wait to tell you what you can't do. More than likely they've made their own compromises in life, and so their opinion comes from their experience. I'm not sure why I listened to these people and why I gave them control over my dream.

That's another reason why it's so important for you to hold on to your vision. The more you define it, the more people will come forward to discourage it. In fact that's probably an indication of how strong your vision is, just count the number of people who try to talk you out of it!

Hold on to Your Dreams

Right after I decided to leave the corporate world I had the opportunity to work on my novel. The way was clear for me to do it and have money to live on while I wrote. But instead of writing I talked myself out of it. I decided that I didn't have the right to be an author or to follow the dream I'd had for years. So, though the door was open for me to walk through, I didn't do it.

My path ended up being a very long one that eventually forced me to face my fears. By running away I'd just ended up running right back into the things I was afraid of. That path also led me back to my writing, though I did take the long way around. If you're struggling right now it's probably because you are not being true to your dream. Though there is a common belief that you have to struggle to have success, you really don't. The struggle usually comes when we resist what comes naturally to us. We aren't listening to our inner guidance or we're fighting to hold on to our limits.

Imagine yourself being weightless. That's what it feels like to not be held down by baggage such as fear and worry. Now imagine yourself flying over the treetops, the buildings and everything else that is holding you back. Your limiting thoughts are the chains and your dream is what is lifting you up. When you are following your dream there may be times when you're not sure of the next step. You may stumble and find out that you made a left when you should've turned right. Your original plans may have to be tweaked a bit to get you back on course. That is all okay and normal. Don't be discouraged because the path has twists and turns or because there are times you can't get the inner critic to be quiet.

Following your dream does not mean you have to lose everything, be homeless or go hungry. It's not a requirement of success. What is true is that most people will not take the action required to get started, or they won't follow through when the next step presents itself. That's when the struggle begins. This is probably why people who don't remain true to their vision are quick to tell others what they cannot do. They're speaking from experience. When you're confronted with that sort of "help" don't take it seriously. Unless they have experience in what they're talking about, their advice isn't based on fact. It's based on assumptions and limiting beliefs. If someone is giving you advice and they have experience, then you can listen—but don't let them drown out your inner voice. Their experience is not the same as yours and you have no idea what their journey was like unless you were there to see it.

Trust your inner guidance and follow your dreams.

"The word 'listen' contains the same
letters as the word 'silent.'"

—Alfred Brendel

GROW

> *"Somewhere, something incredible
> is waiting to be known"*
>
> –Carl Sagan

There's no rule saying that once you start a business you can never do anything else with it. Having your own business gives you the freedom to change when you see new opportunities.

The same applies to projects, hobbies or businesses "on the side" that you may have.

The changes in your business will also reflect the changes going on inside of you. As you evolve and gain confidence you'll set your sights on new things that you want to do and achieve.

Don't feel as though you have to stick to your first choices. As you discover your strengths and find the things that excite you, you'll grow beyond what you initially believed you could do.

છ ૭

Questions to think about…

- What choices have you made and changed?

- Are you comfortable going in new directions when you find other opportunities?

✎ *to journal:* How have you grown in the past year or so?

TRUST YOUR GUT

"Create a definite plan for carrying out your desire and begin at once, whether you're ready or not, to put this plan into action."

–Napoleon Hill

Sometimes it's not easy to find focus. You can reach a point where you know something must be done, you just don't know what. I can spend hours considering this plan or that one. Each alternative makes sense, and yet none of them seems like the way to go.

We can be afraid to commit to an idea or a plan of action because we want to know for sure what the outcome will be.

Often our gut feeling, or intuition is ready to show us the way. It's sort of an early warning system, but so many of us simply ignore it.

There are times when we may rely on a mentor, or someone who appears to have the wisdom that we lack. But there are other times when we know perfectly well what the best course of action is...we just don't follow it.

If you are going in circles about a decision, is it because you can't decide what path to take? Or do you already have a gut feeling about what you want to do, but you don't trust it?

❧ ❧

Questions to think about…

- How many mentors or advisors have you had in your life?

- Do you trust your own guidance when making decisions?

✎ *to journal:* **How often do you trust your intuition?**

PURPOSE

> "We find what we are searching for—or,
> if we don't find it, we become it."
>
> —Jessamyn West

Have you ever wondered if there's something you "should" be doing with your life? When people feel uncertain about things, they start to look at what's going on in their lives. Perhaps the job you've been in for years isn't really what you want to be doing. The career you were once so excited about is now going nowhere. The passion you once felt for your business has burned out and now you're reluctant to try something new.

Some people have always known what they wanted to do with their lives. But I suspect most people have no idea what would make them happy. They've become used to not feeling anything at all, going through their lives like sleepwalkers.

We can spend a lot of time struggling against the current because we believe that things have to be difficult. If they're not difficult some people will create drama in order to make them that way. There is a belief that overcoming obstacles earns you extra points, and it does have a way of teaching you things that can help you in life. However, struggle for the sake of struggle is not very instructive. There has to be a point where you ask if perhaps you're struggling because you're doing the wrong thing.

If you're looking for your purpose, consider what you enjoy doing. What comes easy for you? Chances are the things that are easiest for you are related to your purpose. Is there something that people always ask you to help them with? What brings you joy? Yes, I said joy. That feeling isn't just for special occasions. Unfortunately so many of us are content to spend most of our lives in compromise, settling for "almost good" or "better than nothing" because we don't feel we deserve better. Or we're not sure what we really want because we're not connected to our inner needs and desires. We turn off those whispers by working too much, drinking or engaging in other behavior that will cover up our feelings of dissatisfaction.

Your purpose is what you say it is. It's what makes you come alive. For years I worked in the corporate world putting in long hours and planning my career. Then one day that career path went away as changes rocked the company and put our jobs in jeopardy. I had to think about making my own decisions and not letting them be made for me by default.

It took me a while to come to terms with what I wanted, years as a matter of fact.

All I had to do was let go of the struggle and listen to what had always been calling me.

Deep down you know what you want, all you have to do is get quiet and listen.

ஜ ୡ

Questions to think about...

- Where do you feel that you've been asleep in your life?

- What is calling you?

🖉 *to journal:* **Do you feel you deserve to live a fulfilling life?**

IDENTITY

> " Be who you are and say what you feel
> because those who mind don't matter
> and those who matter don't mind."
>
> —Dr Seuss

Who are you?

Are you living a life created by other people's expectations, or are you deeply, passionately yourself?

We may have to experience many things before we really know who we are. Perhaps we have to go through experiences that shove us up against our deepest fears. Or we may wish and hope for something, only to find that it wasn't what we wanted after all.

It takes courage to release what we've accumulated, to let go of our false identity and step into who we really are.

Are you ready to look into the mirror and see your real self?

ᔥ ⪧

Questions to think about…

- What is your vision for yourself?

- How would you define your identity?

✐ to journal: Have you gone after something only to find that it wasn't really your dream?

REALNESS

"Keep it real."

–Unknown

You hear a lot about being authentic these days. Seems that being "real" and being "true to yourself" are mentioned quite a bit in popular media. Good advice, but what does it really mean?

Contrary to what you may have been told, being "real" doesn't mean you have to be angry or in someone's face. Being true to yourself or "following your bliss" doesn't mean running away from everything in order to satisfy your desires.

So what does it mean?

In truth, each person will define it differently. There's no rule book that will tell you what "realness" means to you.

Only you know the answer to that.

Keep in mind that if you are authentic all the time, it's much less likely that you'll have to use anger to express yourself. Often anger comes from pent-up frustration. It's what happens when your true feelings and desires are not addressed.

Things build up over time, then one day the breaking point is reached. When the explosion comes, it's possible that your truth will be lost and only the blame and anger will remain.

Being authentic can be as simple as being truthful about what you want... and what you don't want. When you keep it real you have absolutely nothing to prove to anyone. Your actions tell the world who you are.

Are you keeping it real?

⅀ ∛

Questions to think about…

- What does it mean to you to be authentic?

- How do you define being "real?"

✎ to journal: **In what way do your actions match your inner beliefs?**

THE MEANING OF LIFE

"Just when I discovered the meaning of life, it changed."
—George Carlin

There comes a time when we start asking questions that don't have easy answers. Why am I here and what am I supposed to be doing with my life?

It may start as a nagging feeling or it may be a deep down yearning for a different type of experience than the one you're having right now.

Some people are searching for their purpose and others are just trying to get through another day. Wherever you're at right now, the meaning of your life is yours to determine.

So how can you tell what your life purpose is? Ask yourself, what makes me happy? What comes easily? What brings me joy?

If you're struggling to find it, stop. The meaning of your life is not in the struggle to be someone you're not; it's in surrendering to who you really are.

℘ ◌

Questions to think about...

- What do you feel is your purpose?

- How often have you felt joy in your life?

to journal: **What activities make you happy?**

YOUR VISION

"Don't give up! Stick to your vision. Here's a big one: If you were given an idea, whether by God or the universe or it came from inside you, remember—that is your vision. It may not have been given to someone else because they can't see it. And you don't have time to wait around for certain people to understand it. When you have a vision and a dream, you have to move on it."

—Taja Sevelle

How has the year been for you so far? Tough, better than expected, or just plain surprising?

Remember that your thoughts form your experience in the world. It's up to you to create a masterpiece.

What's your vision for your life in this moment? When will you start working on your special creation?

Take some time to consider what you want. Is it the same vision that you had earlier this year or last year? If not, what has happened to change it?

If you don't have a vision, write down your thoughts about what you'd like to have in your life. You can bring your dreams to life, but first you have to be honest about what you really want!

∞ ∞

Questions to think about…

- How often do you write down your thoughts and feelings?

- Is your vision right now the same one that you had months or years ago?

to journal: **What do you really want?**

DREAM ON

"That which we do not claim, remains invisible..."

—Marianne Williamson

Have you had a dream that you've put aside? We've all done it at one time or another. Think of how you were when you were younger and the world seemed limitless. We dared to dream without questioning whether those dreams could come true.

Then the years pass, compromises are made and one day there are no more dreams. There is just resignation and bottled up frustration that expands day by day until there is an explosion of illness, depression or rage.

Ever wondered why you have dreams and desires? Do you think you would have them if they were unattainable? Is it enough for you to go through the motions day by day, or are you wanting something much more?

If you dream it you can achieve it. If you desire it you can have it. You only have to be willing to take action to get it. It's not going to fall into your lap, or knock on your door or just show up without effort. You can either spend your life telling yourself what you can't do, or you can just go do it. You don't have to know how it will happen, you only have to believe that it can.

It's your choice.

☙ ☙

Questions to think about…

- What dreams have you put aside?

- Do you look forward to each day or are you anxious and stressed?

to journal: **What's a step you can take in order to bring one of your dreams to life?**

BELIEVE

*"Take the first step in faith. You don't have to see
the entire staircase, just take the first step."*

–Dr. Martin Luther King, Jr.

Even when you know what you want, you can still lose hope when things don't materialize right away. That's when belief becomes extremely important.

When you believe in your dream, you can create miracles. You have to believe in it first, before it manifests and goes from thought to reality. That's very hard to believe because it goes against what a lot of us have been taught.

In the end, it comes down to vision, passion and a desire that is so strong that nothing can stop your dream from becoming real. Even when you don't see evidence, believe. If you can stay focused on your goal, you will reach it.

Not sure that you can maintain your belief?

- Meditate or spend quiet time focusing on your goal.

- Stay away from people who try to discourage you or criticize your dreams.

- Write down your goals and your thoughts about achieving them.

We are all capable of creating our ideal lives and living our dreams. All you have to do is stay focused and believe!

✇ ೞ

Questions to think about…

- What are you passionate about?

- How do you stay focused on your goals?

✎ to journal: **What do you do when you don't see evidence of your dreams becoming real?**

CHAPTER 4: CREATIVITY

"You can't use up creativity. The more you use, the more you have."

—Maya Angelou

When I was a child, my mom gave me a coloring book and crayons. I would spread color all over the page (as opposed to staying within the lines of the pictures). One day my aunt saw my book and said, "you have to stay within the lines." Instead of taking her advice I continued to apply color after color all over the page. Layering colors on top of each other with wild abandon. I didn't think it was fun to stay within the lines or restrict my pictures to nice, neat blocks of color. I use that same philosophy right now when I'm trying to solve a problem or want to come up with a new idea for a product or service. I have to be willing to open up my perspective, otherwise I'll never see the opportunities that may be hidden there.

Even if you don't consider yourself to be an artist, you can use creativity to make leaps and discover possibilities. Consider how you deal with problems or situations where you feel blocked. Do you give up when the usual solutions don't work, or are you willing to try new ways to get around those obstacles?

Often entrepreneurs are going totally out on a limb and do things that have never been done before. They can't rely on past experiences to guide them, so they have to be willing to take chances and follow their gut feelings. This is at the heart of creative brainstorming, which is a very useful tool for discovering possibilities where seemingly none exist.

When you tap into your creativity you'll be surprised at how your perspective can change simply by looking at things in a different way. Don't be afraid to go outside the lines. Open yourself up to limitless possibilities!

Creative Ways to Deal With Doubts

So what happens when you have doubts about your dream? You can see it...most of the time. Other times it seems much too difficult or too far away from your current reality to ever manifest. Perhaps people have told you that you're crazy, or that you aren't the type of person to take such risks. But still your dreams won't let you alone. You try to walk away from them, but they're always in the back of your mind.

Doubt can never destroy a dream, but it can delay your bringing it to life. Every time you say, "this can't happen" you push your dream a bit further away.

So, use creative ways to deal with the doubts when they materialize. Whether it's journaling, creative brainstorming or daydreaming—shifting how you look at the situations in your life will change your results.

- Write down your dreams and ideas in a journal or notebook. Keep them private or share them with your support system. Don't judge them or try to determine how logical they are (or aren't).

- Get quiet and create a vision for what your dream would be like if you were living it right now. Sit down and close your eyes and see the pictures. Feel your emotions. Smell and taste and touch your vision. How does it feel?

- When you feel doubt, ask yourself where this is coming from. Is it a fear of the unknown? Are you feelings based on past disappointments? Do you doubt your dreams because you've been told they're silly or unrealistic?

- Think about the things you've accomplished in other areas of your life. When we're in doubt, we think about our failures, not our successes.

- Accept that it's not important that you know how your dream will manifest. The "how" is not as important as the "what." (As in, knowing what you want.) This is the hardest thing to let go of because it means surrendering control. When you try to control it, we base our expectations on what's happened in the past—not on what's possible in your life right now.

Don't wait for them to disappear before you embrace your dreams; keep believing in them and visualizing them. You'll be surprised at what you will accomplish.

"Lose this day loitering, twill be the same story tomorrow and the next more dilatory. Indecision brings its own delays and days are lost lamenting over lost days. Action-there is courage, magic in it. Anything you can do, or think you can, begin it. Once started, the mind grows heated. Begin the job and the work will be completed."

—Goethe

BALANCE

"I've learned that you shouldn't go through life with a catcher's mitt on both hands. You need to be able to throw something back."

–Maya Angelou

At times there has to be a negotiation between your professional and personal life. Yes, they are both part of one person, but they probably don't have the same priorities. Devoting ourselves solely to our professional needs may mean that an important part of our life is being left out.

What are some ways to negotiate through professional and personal needs?

1. If you are in control of your work hours, set a time to start and stop working.

2. Have time that is strictly family time, friend time or "you" time.

3. Schedule appointments on your calendar for things like going to the gym, pursuing a hobby or volunteering.

4. Don't work endless hours believing that once you've made a certain dollar amount, you'll slow down. You won't. Start now and build the foundation for balancing your professional and personal life.

5. Make your family and friends partners in your success.

⁊ ☙

Questions to think about…

- How do you find balance?

- Would you consider yourself a "workaholic?"

✎ to journal: **How often do you delegate tasks to others?**

HAVING FUN

> *"It's fun to get together and have something good to eat at least once a day. That's what human life is all about—enjoying things."*
>
> –Julia Child

Are you having fun yet?

If you aren't taking time to do something you enjoy, or spending time doing something that gives you energy, you'll burn out. Take a break. Give yourself permission to just be for a few minutes—or a few hours. If there's a lot required of you, you owe it to yourself to recharge those batteries from time to time.

Relax. Refresh. Renew.

❧ ❧

Questions to think about...

- What do you do that gives you energy?

- Is it easy for you to relax and do nothing for a while?

✎ to journal: **When was the last time you took time off from work and responsibilities?**

FLOW

"People, even more than things, have to be restored, revived, reclaimed, and redeemed..."

–Audrey Hepburn

Are you in the flow?

When I'm working on something that I'm really into, I lose track of time. I'm excited and feeling energized.

Years ago when I worked at a job I really disliked, I'd always feel drained. I'd be sitting there at my computer and I could feel the energy pouring out of me. Or I'd have a conversation with someone who was always complaining and I'd feel myself being pulled into the drama.

When you're in the flow you can feel the energy inside of you. You're ready to go out and get things done. You're excited to start your day.

When you're in the flow you bring that energy to everything you do. In turn you can give energy to others, and they pass that energy on to others. It can be that simple. Just by showing up and being connected to your flow you can raise the energy level in everyone you come in contact with.

So, I'll ask again—are you in the flow?

⟠ ⟡

Questions to think about…

- How does it feel for you to be in the flow?

- What activities do you lose yourself in?

✐ to journal: **What drains your energy?**

EXPRESS YOURSELF

> "Sometimes you've got to let everything go...purge yourself. If you are unhappy with anything... whatever is bringing you down, get rid of it. Because you'll find that when you're free, your true creativity, your true self comes out."
>
> –Tina Turner

For many years while I worked in my corporate information technology job, I gave up on my writing. I also stopped my other creative pursuits, such as photography, sewing and piano.

About 10 years into my career, I changed jobs and went to work in a position that required little or no overtime. Finally I had time again to do something other than work, so I decided to add my creative interests back into my life.

After years of neglect, my skills were quite rusty to say the least. When I went back to writing, I enrolled in a series of classes and built my skills back up again.

I reconnected with the joy of expressing myself. My creativity has brought me more satisfaction than I could have imagined. Writing short stories and poems or taking pictures aren't just interests or hobbies, they are a way that I express myself in the world.

Throughout my years in corporate I focused on the goal of advancement. The thought of expressing myself in other ways didn't enter into the equation. I couldn't see how that expression would help me in my career. Unfortunately I didn't realize at that time that I was more than my job. Now I know that we can't close out parts of ourselves and expect to be successful. Success is not just about career advancement. It's about living with meaning and being fulfilled.

Is there something you enjoy doing that you aren't doing?

Are you always putting your creative pursuits off in order to do other work that you think you "should" be doing instead?

What part of your personal self is yearning to be expressed?

Are you ready to bring it out?

☙ ☙

Questions to think about…

- What do you enjoy doing that you aren't doing right now?

- How do you express your creativity?

✐ to journal: **Are you ready to express the positive parts of yourself that have been hidden?**

RECIPE FOR SUCCESS

> *"We have to do the best we can. This is our sacred human responsibility."*
>
> –Albert Einstein

My mom usually makes pies for Thanksgiving. A couple of years ago I wrote some of her recipes down just in case I decided to try them for myself. The reason I haven't used them yet is because I know my pie won't taste the same as hers. We may follow the same recipe, but the result won't be the same. Each person puts something a little different into the thing they're creating.

It might be a bit of a stretch to compare pies to businesses or careers, but in this case I think it's similar. Everyone brings a part of themselves into everything they do. It doesn't matter if there are already other people doing that work—you will bring something to it that no one else can. It also doesn't matter how many other people are in your industry. What you will bring to it will be uniquely your own.

It's easy to get discouraged if we think we can't compete with people who are already doing what we want to do—or we think we are entering a seemingly over-crowded field.

When I was afraid to move forward, I was always finding reasons why I should stay put. Thankfully I didn't let any of them stop me. In the end, it didn't matter who else was already in my field. I'm not in competition with any of them. My knowledge and my experience means I can bring a perspective that no one else will ever have.

So I guess it's okay if my pie doesn't taste like my mom's. Her pie doesn't taste like my grandmother's. Each of us can add something to the mix that is uniquely her own.

❧ ❧

Questions to think about…

- Do you feel that you can't follow your dreams because others are already doing what you want to do?

- Have you ever shared your vision with strangers?

✎ *to journal:* **What are your thoughts about being in competition?**

CHAPTER 5: TAKING RISKS

"When nothing is sure, everything is possible."
—Margaret Drabble

Often people aren't ready to take risks until they feel they have nothing to lose. That can come because of a loss of some kind or an event that wakes us up out of our complacency. The illusion of security is all too comforting, so much so that we can give up everything in order to preserve it.

I say it's an illusion because there's no sure thing. Just because you're getting a regular paycheck doesn't mean it can't go away without warning. Your possessions can disappear in a natural disaster or be taken away. Too often we work at jobs we hate in order to pay for things that we really don't need. Then we sacrifice our true desires in order to continue to pay for more and more things. The big houses and stuff filling the garages give us some sense of place. It's as though the more space we take up with our stuff the more secure we feel. In the end, it's all just stuff. If you've lived a life of compromise because you didn't want to lose your stuff, you'll lose in the end. As they say, you can't take it with you, can you?

When I left the corporate world I didn't realize how much of my identity I had to leave behind. My title and my job function defined me completely. My friends were from work, my income, my entire sense of self was tied to the workplace. My time wasn't my own, seeing how it was regulated by the workplace as well. So when I decided to leave I didn't know what to do next. When my contracting position ended, I was immobile for about two weeks. I simply sat and stared out the window, unable to take any action. For the year I'd worked at the company I'd done my job and actually enjoyed it. I came to think of myself as an important part of the department. I liked the people who sat near my cubicle and regularly ate meals at the nice cafeteria.

When I moved on I realized that though it was a comfortable situation, it wasn't a permanent one. The world kept turning without me. My department got their work done, the people sitting in my section went on with their lives. My identity may have been my job, but what happens when the job goes away? If your sense of importance is tied to a job title and it ceases to exist, what happens to you?

Prior to the contract ending I'd seen a show on TV about a well-known author and how she went to a café to write everyday. I remember thinking how I wish I could do that and how wonderful it must be. Well, once the assignment ended I finally had my chance. Here was my opportunity to do the thing I craved and had wanted for years. But instead of stepping into it, I caved in and went looking for another job.

At that time I was in a position to take the time to write, but I didn't see that. Instead the old programming in my head told me how wrong that was. I couldn't just sit and write all day. That wasn't a real job! Of course when I'd been paid to sit and write during my contracting assignment, the voice hadn't had a problem with that at all. But that was a "real" job in an office, not me following some daydream.

The choices I made were based on fear of taking a risk. Instead of stepping through the open door, I ran to close it. After years of believing that I must work at a job I hated in order to make it, I refused to let go of that belief. I made choices based on my belief that I had to work to make things happen and not pay any attention to my real desires.

I followed other people's advice, no matter how much I didn't agree with it. I didn't trust myself. What did I know? I invested in programs and paid people to help me who I was sure had all my answers. They didn't. In fact in many cases they didn't know much more than I did. My inability to trust myself led me into debt and anxiety over not being able to pay it off. I had simply recreated my corporate environment, except this time I didn't have the regular paycheck. I was frustrated, fearful and angry at myself for getting stuck in the situation. It sounded just like how I felt in my last full-time corporate job.

Finally with my back against the wall I realized I had nothing to lose by focusing on what I wanted. Continuing to do what I didn't want to do wasn't getting me anywhere, so taking a risk didn't feel quite so risky anymore. That is what leads most of us to finally just do it.

Once you realize that the risk isn't quite so risky, it becomes much easier to do what you really want. If you're choosing between financial ruin and the potential for more ruin, that's not much of a risk. Entrepreneurs deal with that risk and that reality all the time. They learn from it, then get up and try again. There really can be no failure unless you stay down. Otherwise, it's a learning experience that teaches you what not to do next time around.

Unfortunately in our culture failure is not looked at so benignly. It is not a learning tool, but a judgment. Winners are put on pedestals, but no one bothers to find out how many failures they had to endure before they won. So, instead the "overnight success" myth or lottery winner mentality is perpetuated. It seems as though you just try something one time then like magic, it all works out with no effort, no stress and no risk. Yes, there have been situations where things have happened for people very easily. But on the back end of their success they've had to deal with how to maintain it. In the end you're going to learn those lessons in one way or another. As long as you want to keep evolving and step out of your comfort zone, you will experience failure. If you're not failing you're not growing, and if you're not failing you're not trying hard enough.

Failing Forward

Making mistakes is another way to learn and grow as you move towards your vision. Learning from mistakes is what really helps (as opposed to repeating the same actions and wondering why things don't work out). Once we learn from what we've done we can make better decisions. Experiencing mistakes may also lead us to find our purpose.

If we're doing things that aren't working, then we're forced to discover why. In the process we may find that we really didn't want to do things that way. Perhaps we were going along for other reasons, or listening to someone else. Failure tells us that we're not on the right track. We may need to tweak a little or to make a major overhaul.

Stepping Out of Your Comfort Zone

This is a big one because for many of us the search for security has become a full-time job. Years ago it may have been possible to find security in a job, but that is no longer the norm. Trusting your intuition comes in very handy here. If we're leaping into something new we have to be able to trust that we're doing the right thing. That assurance can only come when our actions are aligned with our vision.

Having low expectations of what we can achieve can lead to us staying safe—and staying stuck. I've been asked many times by people still in the corporate world if it's possible to work for yourself and duplicate your employee salary. Sure it is, but to be honest, why would you want to? Employee salaries are set by many factors that often have little to do with the quality of the work. Wouldn't you want more once you're in control of what you receive?

Creativity

Taking risks involves many factors, including the ability to be creative. As I mentioned, you have to release the old stories you've been telling yourself if you want to move forward. That means having an open mind for trying new things, and not judging them based on past events.

When you see the big picture you can determine what other factors are involved in your situation. For instance, an entrepreneur may look at overall trends before making a decision about launching a product or expanding a business. Being open to new ideas means they can release pre-conceived notions and try things that may be untried.

Be Uncomfortable

When we try something new we often feel awkward and uncomfortable. This discomfort comes up because we're having a new experience and have nothing to compare it to, or it's like a similar experience we had and we're anticipating the same thing. It's up to us to decide if we're going to react to the discomfort and stay stuck in fear or if we're going to move forward no matter what.

"If you have made mistakes, there is always another chance for you. You may have a fresh start any moment you choose, for this thing we call "failure" is not the falling down, but the staying down."

—Mary Pickford

FEELING STUCK

> *"Don't ask what the world needs. Ask what makes you come alive, and go do it. Because what the world needs is people who have come alive."*
>
> –Howard Thurman

Feeling stuck?

Are you still in a job you dislike or in a relationship that makes you unhappy? Not sure what to do to change your situation? There's one way to be sure you never have the life you want—by doing the same things that you've always done.

So what's one thing you can do to get "unstuck?"

Change your thinking. Your future life does not have to be dictated by what happened in the past. Just because you've had jobs you didn't like doesn't mean you always will. Having bad relationships in the past doesn't mean you're doomed to repeat the heartbreak over and over.

It's up to you how you will live the rest of your life. You make the choice.

What will it be?

- Is there something you'd like to do, but you've been reluctant to start because of past experiences?

- Keep a journal of your dreams and desires for the future. Writing out your thoughts will help you explore the things that may be blocking you.

- See yourself living the life of your dreams. Does if feel possible for you? If not, why not?

- Ask yourself what you get out of staying stuck in your situation. What's the payoff for you?

- Procrastination can be another sign that we're stuck in our thinking. It's a way to pretend we're taking action when we're really not. What are you putting off doing?

- Don't settle for less by assuming that you won't get anything better. That's just an excuse that will keep you stuck in uncomfortable situations. How do you know that you can't get what you really want? Make a commitment to yourself to go after what you desire.

You don't have to stay stuck in a way of life that's no longer satisfying. Make one change today that will take you a step closer to where you want to be.

⚭ ⚬

Questions to think about…

- Where do you feel stuck in you life?

- What's stopping you from having your ideal life?

✐ *to journal*: **Do you believe you have choices in your life?**

MAKING CHANGES IN YOUR LIFE

People are not prepared to be entrepreneurs in school. Instead they're prepared to go into employment and take direction. It is a completely new experience to be responsible for creating your own income or to direct the affairs of your own business. You can't blame your manager when you are the CEO. You can't wait to get an appraisal when you are the one who has to decide if you are doing things correctly or not. This transition is a major change in thinking and living. You will go from someone who may have been dependent on a structure to a person who has to rely on the structure you create. You don't have to ask permission to be yourself. You already have it.

So, let's review what the traits are.

VISION

- Visualize your ideal situation

CREATIVITY

- Stay open to new ways of doing things

INTUITION

- Listen to the voice within

ACTION

- Make a decision and take the next step towards your dream

LOOKING BACK

> *"Gratitude makes sense of our past, brings peace for today, and creates a vision for tomorrow."*
>
> –Melody Beattie

Have you ever felt stuck in the same job situations, relationships or financial circumstances—experiencing the same results over and over?

When you live in the state of "what was" you'll always continue to have the same experiences. Making "what was" into "what is" will insure you'll live in a loop of the same experiences.

Be open to new things coming into your life, but don't assume that you have control over how they will come. When you're open the universe can work freely without being filtered through limited expectations. You won't live from a perspective that says, "what was" must be "what is" and "what will come."

Think about it. If you judge every new situation by what happened in the past, how can anything new enter your life? If it's new and unfamiliar, there's no past experience to base your expectations on. Unfortunately, for some of us the unknown (and unpredictable) must be bad, so as soon as it doesn't fit into our paradigm, we reject it.

Perhaps the fear is that this new job, love interest or financial windfall is really too good for you. It's so different (and so much better) that it must be a mistake. So, you may push it away so that you won't be hurt when it fails. If it doesn't fail, you sabotage it to make sure it conforms to your low expectations.

Then, when the smoke clears and the job, the relationship or your finances are in ruins, you complain about how you wouldn't have any luck if you didn't have bad luck. Poor you, you're just one of those people who always gets the short end. That's your story and you're sticking to it, right?

The person you are now is not the person you were. The knowledge you have today came because you went through those prior experiences. Don't beat yourself up about what you "should" have done. You did the best you could with the knowledge you had at the time.

If you want to have new experiences, learn from the past and then release it.

∾ ☙

Questions to think about...

- Are you beating yourself up over things you've done in the past?

- Have you ever felt that you don't deserve good thing to happen to you?

🖉 to journal: **Are you reluctant to try new things?**

PERSPECTIVE

"Preconceived notions are the locks
on the door to wisdom."

—Merry Browne

This is a little story about changing your perspective. The water in my bathroom sink used to drain out very slowly. When I opened the stopper, the water would sit and slowly swirl for what seemed like hours (though it really wasn't that long). Every time I used the sink I would be annoyed that the water didn't drain properly.

Since the sink also didn't hold water for very long (the stopper didn't work) I assumed that the slow drain had something to do with the stopper mechanism located in the drain. So, I lived with it until one day my mom suggested using drain cleaner. I was sure the problem was mechanical, so I was skeptical. It took me about a week to finally pour some drain cleaner down the drain. About a half hour later I stopped up the sink and filled it with water. When I unstopped the sink, the water immediately drained out.

I was sure I knew the answer to the problem with the sink, so I didn't even bother to investigate other solutions. Isn't that the way life usually is? We tolerate conditions in our lives, grow annoyed and frustrated—so sure that we can do nothing to change the situation. Then one day we try something new, look at the problem from a different direction and there's the answer.

Thinking that we know it all can be a trap. We're so sure of the outcome that we eliminate all other possibilities. Our options are only limited by our beliefs.

℘ ℂℛ

Questions to think about…

- Have you ever found a solution to a problem by changing your perspective?

- How often do you put yourself in a position to learn new things?

✎ *to journal*: **What new things have you learned over the past year?**

FEAR OF CHANGE

> *"Some people change when they see the light, others when they feel the heat."*
>
> –Caroline Schoeder

Change is always happening around us. Though the events in our everyday lives may seem constant, nothing really stays the same.

Often we're going through the motions, following old habits or familiar patterns without realizing it. Have there been times when you've wanted to do something different? Have you wanted to make a change and talked yourself out of it?

Ask yourself, is it fear of change or is it fear of the unknown? Or is it the loss of being in control that is the real fear?

For some people, trying something new is exhilarating, for others it is frightening. It all depends on your perspective.

You may feel discomfort when trying new things, but that's to be expected. Often you may find that the fear is really based on what you believe will happen, opposed to what really is possible.

Fear can also be a way for us to stay stuck if we use it as an excuse not to take action.

1. Is your fear based on fact or on a possible outcome?

2. What's the worst that can happen?

✍ ✑

Questions to think about…

- Do you like being in control?

- If you've had an experience where you weren't in control of a situation, how did it feel?

✎ to journal: **How often has fear stopped you from taking action?**

RISK IT

> *"All our dreams can come true, if we*
> *have the courage to pursue them."*
> —Walt Disney

You know when it's time to make a change. You can feel the desire for a different kind of life, and you know what you're doing right now is not fulfilling. It's not an easy decision to make, but in the end, you have to consider if you want to stay in a place that will drain your energy and your hopes with each passing day, or take a risk.

Having low expectations of what we can achieve can lead to us staying safe—and staying stuck.

When you decide to take a risk you've made a decision to break through what you thought was possible up to that point. You're going into unfamiliar territory with no idea what will happen after you start out. For some people, this is not only uncomfortable, it's impossible. They'll take a step, then pull back once the anxiety level rises and they realize that they don't have the security of knowing what to expect.

Living in familiar habits is easy—even if they're negative they're still familiar. Stepping out when you can't see what you are stepping into is hard. It takes courage and faith that when you do step out, there will be something solid to support you.

It takes belief in yourself and a willingness to get back up again if (and when) you fall down. The one sure way to break through your limiting beliefs is to take a risk.

ℴ ℭ

Questions to think about…

- What risks have you taken to achieve your dreams?

- How difficult is it to leave the familiar for the unfamiliar?

to journal: **Do you have habits that you dislike, but are reluctant to stop doing?**

CHANGES

> "We can't solve problems by using the same kind of thinking we used when we created them."
>
> –Albert Einstein

Change is not impossible, though there are times when it may seem that way. It's easy to give up because it can feel excruciating. So much has to be released that you wonder what will be left of you when it's all over.

When you're experiencing change, ultimately you must release the parts of your life that no longer serve you. Unfortunately we can end up struggling to stay in control because it's unsettling to step into new experiences. We live from our perceptions of reality. My reality will probably not be the same as yours because we filter our current experiences through the experiences we've already had. If we aren't open to thinking differently (and hold on to our expectation that life will always be what it always has been) there can be no change.

By controlling what we experience, we insure that nothing new or unexpected will ever enter into our lives. If something new does enter, we make every effort to force it back out again. Often this effort is unconscious. We don't even realize we're doing it. Instead we make rationalizations about why the person, place or thing is not right for us.

We hold on to what is familiar, even if it causes us pain. Suppose something new and different comes into our lives and gets our hopes up? What happens if it disappoints us? Better to stay in control, limit our exposure to new and unpredictable experiences and protect ourselves from being hurt. Staying safe can also keep us in a cycle of pain.

❧ ❧

Questions to think about…

- How do you handle changes in your professional and personal life?
- Have you stopped taking chances because of past experiences?

to journal: **Do you dislike being in situations that you cannot control?**

WHAT DO YOU KNOW?

> *In a world of change the learners will inherit the earth, while the learned will find themselves beautifully equipped for a world that no longer exists."*
>
> –Eric Hoffer

It's really frustrating to try to explain something to someone and all they say is, "I know, I know." If they know, why do they need an explanation? It becomes an immediate response to pretend that you know something even when you don't. Perhaps it's fear of looking stupid, or being wrong...or being vulnerable.

No one has all of the answers—even if they think they do. Admitting to what you don't know will leave you open to learning and growing. Being sure you know everything, and closing off your mind to new ideas will keep you stuck.

Some people "don't know that they don't know." Others "know that they don't know" and want to learn. Which type of person are you?

℘ ℭ

Questions to think about…

- Are you open to new things or do you feel you know it all already?

- How do you feel when you deal with people who aren't listening to what you're saying?

✐ *to journal:* **Is it easy to admit when you don't know something?**

APPEARANCES

"The world can only change from within."

–Eckhart Tolle

A couple of times a week one of my neighbors takes his leaf blower and blows the debris from the front of his house. However, the rear of his house has a year's worth of leaves piled up—along with various other things. Another neighbor cuts the lawn in front of his home, but on the side of the house the grass is knee high.

In life we can be so concerned with appearances that we don't bother to maintain anything that can't be seen by others. As long as the surface is bright and shiny, it's all good.

If we hide who we are in order to project an image of what we are not, then we're keeping up appearances. Sweeping the dust under the bed or pushing the leaves into a back corner of the yard is really no different than hiding our issues under a mask of "everything's okay." It may look fine on the outside, but on the inside it's a mess.

I've also done the same thing. A pile of mail was on my dining room table for several weeks. I kept putting off cleaning it up because, as you know, cleaning up clutter is a totally tedious task. So, finally I just picked up the entire pile and put it into a chair. It's not cluttering up the table anymore, and now things look neat and tidy. But when I have to move the chair, or walk by it, that pile of mail is a reminder of what I've left undone. Not to mention that it's a drain on my energy because I have to keep pretending it isn't there.

We can't have things together if we have stuff hidden away. If you feel that you have to hide it, there must be something that makes you uncomfortable about it being seen. When we keep up appearances we're putting on a face that doesn't match who we really are.

A lot of us have been made to believe that we aren't good enough, so we hide the parts of ourselves that we're not comfortable with. We're bombarded with messages telling us that we have to fix this or that part of ourselves. Our teeth aren't white enough, our bodies not thin enough, our houses not big enough—the list goes on. Real change can't happen if we are covering up disorder with a mask of perfection. It happens when we take responsibility for our actions and we accept ourselves just as we are.

⟡ ⟡

Questions to think about…

- Does your outside appearance match who you are inside?

- What do you feel that you cannot reveal to others?

✎ to journal: **Do you behave differently when other people are watching?**

CHANGE IN DIRECTION

> "You only live once, but if you do
> it right, once is enough."
>
> Mae West

Why do we stay in bad situations? If you're feeling disgusted, angry or frustrated, then you know what I'm saying. Or maybe it hasn't gotten that far yet. Perhaps you're just tired, bored and feeling like you could be doing something else with your life.

I've been there plenty of times. There's a point where you know you're not happy, but you keep going through the motions because it's easier than calling it quits.

We stay long past the time when we should have left, then we end up rationalizing why we're staying. If we want to move on, we have to prepare for it.

In my last corporate job I procrastinated about making a career transition. My new career was not going to just show up at my house and knock on the door. I had to at least meet it halfway. Instead I tried to talk myself into staying where was, because after all, it wasn't that bad. I was getting paid. So what if the environment was negative and I felt stifled, was it really going to be different somewhere else?

Sometimes we procrastinate because we aren't ready to make a change. Even though I disliked by job situation, it was familiar. It's strange how we can be unhappy with a situation and yet comfortable with it at the same time.

Although it's human nature to wait until we're forced to take action, it's not the best course to take. I've done that enough to know that in the end, it's not worth it.

What I've learned (finally) is that it's better to move towards something than to be running away from something. When you know when to leave, you get to decide where you are going.

ড়ে ভ

Questions to think about...

- What is your next step in your life?

- Are you procrastinating about something right now?

✐ to journal: **What actions have you taken that have brought you closer to your goals?**

NEUTRALIZE

*"Innovation distinguishes between
a leader and a follower"*

—Steve Jobs

I was watching a real estate program where a realtor was telling a seller that her home was too unique. Her bedroom was "undefined" because it had a divider between the bedroom and the closet, the kitchen tiles were too busy, and the driveway was too long.

Meanwhile, the property was beautiful and the views were fantastic. It didn't matter; all that mattered was that her home was not plain enough to appeal to most people.

On another show, the realtor walked through saying, "neutralize" whenever she saw a wall with a hint of color. I thought I was watching Star Trek. Set those photon torpedoes on "neutralize!" (No, they never said that on Trek, not that I know of anyway.)

When I graduated from high school, I was told I should be a lawyer, a doctor, an engineer, etc. Being a writer never came up. Neither did having my own business. All I was supposed to do was get a good job and get a pension.

Feeling pressure not to follow your own unique path? Just fall into line, get into that cubicle and keep quiet. You're getting paid, aren't you? Not being in a cubicle isn't bad, but it's not for everyone. Beige walls and generic tile floors aren't for everyone either.

Find out what appeals to you, then do it. Neutralize the wall colors in your house if you must, but don't do that to your life.

& ∞

Questions to think about...

- What path are you following?

- Do you feel pressure to go along with what others want for you?

to journal: **How often have you felt compelled to fit in?**

CHAPTER 6: DECISIONS

"To live creatively free, do what you know how to do now then 'act as if' you know how to do the rest."

—Sark

In this success trait we find the most important quality of successful people—making the decision to manifest your vision. You won't achieve anything if you aren't willing to take that step.

It is important to believe you can manifest your desires in spite of what you see around you in this moment. Hold the vision for what you want and make the decision to move forward.

There's something deeply disturbing about giving up the things that we are comfortable with. Even if we're not terribly happy with our situation, there can be a certain comfort in knowing what to expect day after day. A reason for that is because our sense of self is wrapped up in a certain way of life.

We are much more than what we do during working hours, just as we are much more than the names we've been given. We are also much more than our physical appearance, our ethnicity, skin color, age or sexual orientation. Deep down we are more complex than even we can realize. Our lives are the sum of our experiences, and each of these experiences has given us a story about who we think we are.

No doubt you've heard that people live from their perceptions, or that perception is reality. Our perception...our story is what we live through. It defines us. It's the roadmap we look at to tell us where we are and what is happening around us.

In the end, we cannot change the world to suit us. However we can change how we respond to the world.

Where Does it Begin?

Where we run into trouble is when we allow those stories to become part of our identity. I've met many people who say that they can't write, or they hate writing. I'd guess that somewhere in that person's past they were made to feel that their writing wasn't good enough. So, they accepted that story as their reality. The same is true for people who have been told they are stupid, or ugly or not quite good enough to be successful.

In the workplace, if we are defined by a job title, a salary or a grade level, it becomes part of our identity. The people we associate with, the economic class we belong to, the neighborhood we live in, the car we drive...it can all be tied to what it means to be that type of person. There is a certain comfort in knowing what to expect—even if you hate your situation. The prospect of starting over from zero can be very frightening.

When you decide to make a change in your life, you are starting on a journey of discovery. You will be made to pull off layer after layer of the stories and beliefs that you've held for years.

Sooner or later we'll have to address the part of ourselves that we suppressed so that we could live according to our stories. When that happens, it becomes impossible for us to pretend to be what we are not. That's when the work begins. Going through that experience enables us to discover who we really are.

A big reason why people stay stuck is because if they believed something 20 or 30 years ago they still want to hold on to it in the present time. When they're faced with conflicting situations, they refuse to accept the new programming and continue to hold to their beliefs. This keeps them stuck because they refuse to take responsibility for their decisions and choose to blame outside events that they cannot control. If you can only be happy when outside events are to your liking, then you will rarely be happy. Some people would rather stay stuck in fear, anger and frustration and blame everything (and everyone) else than to make a decision that may take them in a different direction.

Their old story blocks a new story from being written, and so they continue to experience the same events over and over. What they believed at age 10, 20, 40, 50 and beyond never deviates. Why this fear? Because by releasing their story they may have to also release their identity and create a new one. This can feel as though you are being taken apart piece by piece, but creation requires destruction first. To let the new in, the old must be released. If you are holding tight to what you have in a vain attempt to never lose it, you will be closed to anything new entering your experience.

Without making a decision and taking action nothing will occur. Or rather, things will continue happen to you as opposed to you being a conscious participant in your own life.

"Most of the shadows of this life are caused by standing in one's own sunshine."

Ralph Waldo Emerson

Why It's Not Easy

It would be nice if we could go through these experiences and come out of them completely changed forever. Unfortunately that is not the case. We still have to live in the world surrounded by people who may still be rooted in fear and apprehension when it comes to making a change. We may also be influenced by negative media and be in environments that don't support our making changes.

If you don't maintain the changes you've made, you will eventually start to slip into your old behaviors. It will happen without your consciously realizing it—which is the problem When we're not in the moment and we're either anxious about the future or are fretting over the past, we open ourselves up to falling back into the old behaviors.

So, what should we do? Stay focused on the present moment. Don't project yourself forward in order to find something to worry about. At the same time, don't beat yourself up over what you "should" have done in the past.

Instead stay in this moment. Something else you can do if you feel yourself losing your focus is to step into your vision for what you really want. Creating the vision and forgetting about it is not an option. Visualize it as often as you can. Write about it and be sure to fill in the experience as much as possible. You want to feel as though you are in that situation now.

Staying focused on your vision is tough if things aren't going well in the present. If you're being challenged, it can be next to impossible to stay focused on a vision and not give your attention to what's falling apart around you. However, you must believe even when there's no visible evidence that you are about to manifest your dreams. This is what makes it all hard to do. We've been conditioned to trust outside conditions more than we trust ourselves. It doesn't feel natural to trust in our vision first and the results second.

Trusting Yourself

The key here is trust. Trust yourself and believe in your vision even when there's no evidence of it happening yet. This can be very difficult to do because we may have an expectation of when we want things to happen. If they don't come to pass according to our own time clock, we may end up believing it will never happen. Often when we're about to lose faith in change ever coming is exactly when it arrives.

Though it may not come the way we expected, however, and so we can end up not recognizing opportunities when they appear.

None of this is easy because we have to continually stay focused while keeping our doubts and fears (and naysayers) at bay. During this time is when we can learn a lot about ourselves because we are confronting our deepest anxieties. This is the challenge and can lead to our most satisfying successes.

PERFECTION

"It is the greatest of all mistakes to do nothing because you can only do a little."

–Sydney Smith

Looking for perfection?

Sometimes we believe that things must be perfect before we take action. We can stay in planning mode forever. Tweaking here, revising there, thinking about it, thinking about it again, researching, etc.

There's nothing wrong with being prepared, but if all the preparations never lead to action, then what are we preparing for?

Set a date for completion, and work towards that goal. When you get to your "due date," go for it!

❧ ❦

Questions to think about…

- How is perfectionism affecting your life?

- Have you set due dates for your important goals?

✎ to journal: **Do you ever get stuck in planning and preparing mode?**

GOALS

"You got to be careful if you don't know where you're going, because you might not get there."

–Yogi Berra

If you want to change for the better, then you have to believe in it. You have to be there on the inside long before you see the outside results. Instead of focusing on what you don't have, think about what you want to accomplish.

Do you want a new job, or to return to school or to move to a new place? What steps are you taking to make those things happen?

1. Write down your ideas for the future. Don't edit—just write whatever comes to mind.

2. On another page, write down your thoughts about where you feel you are right now.

3. Use another page to list the steps you can take to get from where you are to where you want to be. Again—don't edit, just write.

Trust yourself and let your ideas flow.

⅏ ⅍

Questions to think about...

• Is it difficult to believe before you see evidence?

• How often have you trusted your own feelings?

to journal: **What steps are you taking to reach your goals?**

CONTROL

"I can do anything but I can't do everything."
—Unknown

Have you ever put pressure on yourself to be perfect at everything you do?

Have you ever been angry with yourself for not knowing how to do something—even if you've never done it before?

Do you feel you always have to be responsible because you can't trust that someone else will do the job as well as you can?

How about giving yourself a break? Just because you can do anything doesn't mean you have to do everything yourself. Knowing when to ask for help is important.

I'm a big-picture person with little patience for details. I'm also a perfectionist at heart who is reluctant to let go of control. So what to do?

I released control and hired a virtual assistant to help me with administrative tasks. Now I can focus on my coaching, writing and interviewing my internet radio show guests. I can do what I love to do, and be better for everyone I interact with.

Yes, I can do anything I set my mind to...but I don't have to do everything.

Make a list of tasks that you struggle doing. Is there a way to delegate them to someone else?

Perhaps perfectionism is getting in the way. It's much better to get things done than to wait until they can be done perfectly.

∞ ∞

Questions to think about...

- Do you feel that you must do everything?

- How often do you ask for help when you need it?

to journal: What tasks do you dislike doing and which ones do you love?

DRAMA

"Few of us write great novels; all of us live them."

–Mignon McLaughlin

Do you spend a lot of time being influenced by someone else's drama? Are energy vampires draining you and leaving you exhausted?

Life can be challenging at times, but all drama all the time is not required. If someone in your environment is always coming to you with their problems, their negative viewpoint or the latest episode of their personal soap opera don't be pulled into their story.

How we live our lives can't be determined by outside events—or people. If we allow that to happen, our sense of self will always be directed by what's going on outside of us. We will be in permanent react mode instead of setting our own pace.

Are you living from your core beliefs and feelings, or are you always riding on a roller coaster of emotions, pulled along by outside events and people?

You make the choice.

❧ ☙

Questions to think about…

- Are you holding on to stories from your childhood experiences?

- What words do you use to describe yourself?

✎ to journal: **Do you have behaviors that you'd like to change?**

WHAT DO YOU WANT?

"Too many of us are not living our dreams because we are living our fears."

—Les Brown

Do you know what you want? Have you ever asked yourself, "What do I want to get out of this situation?" If it's a job or an opportunity, a relationship—do you know what you really want?

There are times when I find myself just going along with what I think is the next logical step. Years ago I was working at Lucent and I wanted to transition to a technical writing job from a computer programmer job. I never thought about why I wanted that new type of position. I just figured it would be a way to move out of information technology.

What I realized later is that I didn't want to be a technical writer. It seemed easier to go for what I thought I could get, as opposed to what I really wanted.

What do you really want?

Do you think it's possible?

What are some of your goals? Write them down in a journal. You can set up a timeline for when you'd like to accomplish them, so you can stay on track. Once you start making changes you may find that your goals will change as you change.

∾ ∾

Questions to think about...

- What do you feel is possible in your life?

- How often do you write down your goals?

to journal: Have you ever switched paths because you changed your mind about what you wanted?

YOUR STORY

"Know thyself."

–Socrates

What's your story?

Have you ever said, "that's just how I am," to explain away behavior you'd rather not change?

If you are not living the life you want, is there a story you've created that explains why you can't have it?

Too old, too young, too thin, too fat, lack of education, too much education, not knowing the right people, knowing too many of the wrong people...etc.

There's always a story. The story is not who we are, it's the script we create for ourselves to live by. But at some point, we have to stop and consider if that story is actually true.

Some people define themselves by their childhood experiences, others by how their parents or family feel about them. Still others define themselves by their accomplishments in the world, or their failures.

If you were to strip away all of the stuff that has accumulated along the way, how would that feel?

Put down the script. Whatever you want to accomplish in business, career...in life...it can't happen if you are not in touch with who you are beneath the story.

⅋ ⳺

Questions to think about...

- How many mentors or advisors have you had in your life?

- Do you trust your own guidance when making decisions?

to journal: **How often do you trust your intuition?**

SURRENDER

"Every act of creation is first an act of destruction."

–Pablo Picasso

When you can't see what's ahead of you, it's easier to hold on to what you already have. Even if your current situation is painful, you know what to expect from it. But change will come, whether you initiate it or not.

In the beginning you'll be resistant when you try something new. That's why change must start with the way we think about ourselves. Only then can we reinforce our new thoughts with action. At first it will be difficult, uncomfortable even. If we don't see immediate results from the changes, it'll be easy to believe that we're wasting our time.

However, if we're currently dissatisfied with some aspect of our lives, we're already in the process of change. Awareness means that some part of us has changed, and we're no longer comfortable with the status quo.

There's no change without surrender. Surrender the need to be in control. Surrender the illusion of security. Surrender and move through the fear that keeps you stagnating in a life you've outgrown.

ॐ ∞

Questions to think about...

- How has your awareness changed as you've gone through your life?

- What have you surrendered?

to journal: Is fear holding you back from something you really want?

CHAPTER 7: TAKE ACTION

"What people say you cannot do, you
try and find that you can."
—Henry David Thoreau

So, how do you start using these success traits in your life? It may seem difficult at first to adjust to a new way of thinking, but like anything it will take practice. You have to be willing to keep going even when things seem difficult or you have no visible evidence that there are any changes happening. This is what separates those who are successful from those who spend their lives dreaming about it.

Create Your Vision

Begin by sitting in a quiet place and closing your eyes. Set aside time for yourself so that you can go within and really visualize your dream.

Picture your ideal career, job, business, love, new home…put yourself in the middle of it. Engage all of your senses, not just seeing but tasting, feeling, smelling—all of your senses. Allow yourself to experience everything without judgment. Don't think about whether this is really possible, or criticize yourself for having these desires. Just let the pictures unfold and accept that this is what you really want.

Start off with five minutes, then 10, then 15 minutes at a time. Do this everyday. Once you have the vision defined, get a notebook and write down what you're seeing and feeling. Pretend it's one year in the future and you're writing about what has happened now that your vision has become real. Describe the entire experience as though you were writing to a friend about how things are now that you are living this ideal life.

If you ever have cause to doubt, go back to your letter and reread it. Feel free to tweak it and make changes if you desire. It is perfectly normal to find that your original thoughts give way to something else once you allow yourself to dream. It's like peeling away layers—you go you may find there are desires that you had no idea were hidden there.

Be honest with yourself about what it is you want., otherwise, you'll have conflicting desires and your results will be just as conflicted.

Be Creative

In order to be open to thinking outside of the box you have to be open to thinking in different ways. What you believed at one time may not apply in your new situation. If you're not open to accepting new information, then it will be difficult for you to believe in things that are outside of your current (or past) experience.

Even if you don't consider yourself to be creative, there is creativity in all of us. Imagination is not just for children! If you've ever daydreamed, or created something new you have used your imagination. Look around you. Everything you see was once an idea in someone's mind. You also have the ability to dream and to create.

So how do you get those creative juices flowing? Here are some suggestions.

"Free write"—Take five or ten minutes to write anything that comes to mind. Don't edit, just write for the allotted time. What you'll find after a while is that you'll be reluctant to stop when the time is up!

Become an artist—Try watercolor painting, drawing or finger painting! Just have fun with it and don't worry about being perfect. It's just for your own enjoyment. Once you release the need to be perfect and go with whatever you are feeling, you are making room for your creativity to flourish.

Learn something new—Have you ever wanted to learn a language or take up a new hobby? Go to the library and check out books or audios. Enroll in an adult school course at your local high school, community college or find a course online. Take a different route home from the store or from work. Get out of your everyday routine.

You don't have to make major changes all at once. When you take small steps you'll find it will be much easier to explore new ideas and opportunities.

Listen to Your Intuition

We all have an inner guidance system called our intuition. We've all had situations where our inner voice may have warned us not to take an action, and we did it anyway. Or we were led to do something that turned out perfectly for us. Unfortunately we often end up trusting the judgment of others before we trust our own. In fact, we may not even hear our intuition speaking to us because there are so many other voices coming at us, telling us what to do.

In order to hear our intuition we need quiet, and for some of us that is not very easy to come by. There are televisions in elevators, advertisements on shopping carts, signs everywhere vying for our attention. In a world where we are constantly bombarded, how can we find a quiet place?

If you want to hear your inner voice, then you have to find the quiet time whenever you can. Ideally you should start out the day with quiet meditation of some kind. If it's a few moments sitting in your car, at your desk or in the shower, take the time to listen.

Clear your mind—Instead of going over your to-do list, clear the mental clutter and don't think about anything for a moment or so. It'll be a challenge at first, but give it a try.

Ask yourself what you want—How often do you ask yourself what you want? Now is the time.

Listen—Now, listen for the answer. Perhaps you'll hear words or see pictures—it doesn't matter how it comes. You may not get the answer right away, but it will come if you give yourself the quiet time to hear what your own inner voice is saying.

It will be difficult to maintain a vision if you are not basing it on your true desires. That is why it's so important that you know what you want, and are able to separate it from what you think you should want (or what others want for you). The more you come to trust this inner guidance system, the more you will find that you can trust yourself and require less validation from outside of yourself.

Take Action

In the end it doesn't matter if you have great ideas if you don't take any action to bring them into reality. When it comes to action, however, you have to trust your own judgment as to what is the right step to take. Action doesn't mean just running around in all directions. It means taking the next best step to bring you closer to what you want to manifest.

For instance, if you have an idea but don't know how to make it happen you would check with your inner guidance system. Perhaps you'll get an idea to call someone you recently met at a networking event, or you'll be led to check out a specific website or go to a certain place. The important thing to do is to follow through and take that action.

Often we become afraid when we consider that we can really live our dreams. If we've believed that we can't have what we want, or we don't deserve it, it can grip us in fear to accept the idea that we can have it. This can lead us to freeze up and never move beyond that place of fear. Then we can end up giving up and falling into bitterness and resentment.

Have you ever felt resentful or envious of someone else who seemed to have it made? It's very possible that that person is doing what you really want to do, but for whatever reason you've stopped yourself from doing it. So, instead of stepping out there ourselves, we become angry at others who are doing what we wish we could do. Don't let yourself fall into that trap! Once you take action and move forward in spite of the fear, you will insure that you will continue to step into opportunities where others see nothing but obstacles.

Now It's Your Turn!

Take a few moments to write down your thoughts about what you've read. Go through each of the success traits and consider how you feel about each one. When have you used them in your life? How do you feel you can apply them going forward? What are your dreams for the future? What desires have you had that you have not acknowledged up to this point?

It's time to take action and realize your dreams. Don't feel that you have to work on bringing them all to life at one time. Pick one thing—the most important thing to you right now—and start there. This is your time to connect with your power so that you can create your vision, tap into your creativity and follow your inner guidance so that you'll know the next action to take. It's time to shift your thinking and create your ideal life!

BEGINNING

"The secret of getting ahead is getting started."
Sally Berger

Have you ever had a project you wanted to work on, but were reluctant to start?

I have a few writing projects that I keep putting off. Though I have the ideas and the desire, I can't get myself to start working on them. Is it the fear of failure? Or maybe I'm afraid of being overwhelmed once I've started the project. Whatever the reason, thinking of starting a project can be very stressful.

Sometimes it's the fear of failure that stops me. Suppose my writing project doesn't turn out the way I'd hoped? Maybe once I start writing, the words won't come or the piece won't be as good as I thought. If it's a project like clearing clutter, then I usually put it off because it seems so tedious. So the project sits and sits, and the more I think of it, the larger the task becomes.

So how do you begin? It may sound trite, but you begin by making a start. You take one step, then another. Set a date on the calendar, or a time to work on that particular task. Set a beginning time and an end time. When the time is up, then stop and move on to something else. Often when I do that, I end up wanting to continue. The project (once I got started) wasn't as daunting as I'd thought.

Take one step forward. You may be surprised at how much progress you make.

₧ ₙ

Questions to think about...

- How easy is it for you to start a new project?

- Do you want everything to be perfect before you begin?

✎ to journal: **Has fear of failure ever stopped you from working on something you really wanted to do?**

BECOMING AN ENTREPRENEUR

Entrepreneurial traits can certainly be used by employees and entrepreneurs alike, but there's also some other advice for entrepreneurs-to-be. If you're reading this and you want to use the success traits in your new business, there are some steps that I recommend.

Back when I was in corporate as a full-time employee I found it next to impossible to start a business while I was employed. I regularly had 10-hour workdays and sometimes had to work on weekends and holidays. Once I became a contractor, my time was much more manageable and I could work on my business on my off hours. There are many "employee moonlighters" juggling full-time work and a business. Though I wouldn't recommend doing it for a very long time (you'll get burned out fairly quickly trying to work around the clock) it is a way to get started and have less risk.

Even if you have the ability to put in hours on the job and in your business, eventually you will have to make the transition into being a full-time entrepreneur if you want your business to grow. Otherwise your side business will remain just that, and you will never reach the potential that you dreamed of.

What you need is a plan to move into your position as CEO. Getting that regular paycheck can be very reassuring and provides a feeling of security that will be hard to give up. Having a timeline will keep you on track and give you the motivation you need to keep moving forward.

If you are unemployed at this time, don't feel that you can't start a business. Depending on where you live there may be programs to assist unemployed professionals who want to make the transition. So, don't rule anything out until you've looked into your options! Take a look at the "For More Information" section for websites and books that will give you some inspiration.

What are some steps to follow in order to prepare for starting a business?

1. Set the date—decide when you would like to move into running your business full-time. Six months from now? Three months? One year? Set a date that feels comfortable for you.

2. Look at your finances—once you have your date, work backwards from there and determine what has to happen financially. For instance, do you need a certain amount of money for business expenses or to launch a new product? Once your salary is no longer coming in, how long will it take for your business income to fill that gap? Be honest about your expenses and how much money you need to cover them. Now would be a good time to research funding options such as angel investors, grants or loans. If you

get any loans from family members write up an agreement so that things are done in a professional manner. You don't want misunderstandings to dominate if things don't go according to plan.

3. Trim the fat—start eliminating as much personal debt as possible. You may need to incur additional debt to put into your business, so get rid of as much as you can while you still have a regular salary.

4. Communicate—let your family know what your plans are for leaving your day job. Everyone has to be on the same page and know what is expected of them when the transition happens. It's best to discuss any concerns now—don't wait until you've left your job and then have to deal with issues around your decision.

5. Prepare for unpredictability—once you are responsible for creating and managing your own income, it is not the same as living with a paycheck coming in on a regular (and predictable) schedule. There will be fluctuations in your income (not to mention the different types of taxes and expenses involved). Take this time to do your research so you'll be prepared.

6. Don't wait to network—depending on your business, being a full-time entrepreneur can mean spending much more time alone as opposed to being in an office environment. Start networking and connecting with other entrepreneurs so you can build a support system before you go out on your own.

7. Create your vision—get clear about your vision for what you want to accomplish. Your business will be a reflection of you and your beliefs about yourself. Limiting beliefs will impact your business success. If you're optimistic and stay open to opportunities, your potential will be unlimited.

8. Do your research—determine your target market (who your customers are) and define your ideal customer. The more work you do ahead of time will mean less problems later on. Don't wait until you have launched your business before you discover whether there's a market for what you're selling.

9. Get your tools—pick out software you'll need for accounting and record keeping. Set up a filing system so you won't have to scramble to find important papers at tax time.

10. Trust yourself—there are a lot of "gurus" in the entrepreneurial world who make claims about their programs and services. You should hire a mentor or business coach to assist you in your start up, however, you should also be discerning about who you hire. Set up a budget for training and materials and stick to it. Be skeptical of claims that sound too good to be true. Building a business will require effort and focus. Offers promising you big rewards with low risks are usually little more than hype. Don't get into the pattern of chasing the latest thing, instead focus on making progress step by step.

SHOWING UP

> *"Though you've broken your vow a thousand times, come, come again."*
>
> —Rumi

Do you ever find yourself frustrated because you're always starting and stopping something? For instance, that diet program that never seems to last past the first week. Or the exercise program that you were excited about when you started. Or the vow to finally clear clutter that ended after you realized how big a mess you have in your garage...or your closet...or in your car.

Don't beat yourself up. For those of us who dislike details but love seeing the "big picture," the thought of slogging through the grunt work is not very appealing.

We have good intentions, we can see the finish line, and we know how great it will feel to finally reach it. Then, we run out of steam.

Work, or other obligations get in the way, and we don't follow through.

Have you ever heard the saying, "try, try again?" Well, that's great advice. Success doesn't come from doing things perfectly; it comes from getting up when you've fallen down. Each time you get up you're a bit wiser and more determined to get to the end result you've envisioned.

You'll make it. Just keep going. It's only a little bit farther to success.

ঙ ০ঙ

Questions to think about...

- Have you ever been stopped by failure?

- What successes have you enjoyed in your life?

to journal: **What usually motivates you to keep going when you want to quit?**

ACTION

> "Most people confuse wishing and wanting with pursuing. You must place your trust in action."
>
> —Price Pritchett

I'm one of those people who have to think a lot about something before I take action. I'll look at it from this angle, or that angle. I'll buy a lot of books on the subject, listen to CD's, attend teleclasses—gather as much information as possible before I make a decision.

There's nothing wrong with doing research, but at some point the research has to end so that the action can begin. Have you ever planned to do something, then you look up a week later, a month later, a year later and it still hasn't been done?

Sometimes we don't take action because we really don't want to do whatever it is. It may seem like a good idea, but when we think about actually doing it, we'd rather not.

Unfortunately many times we really desire something, but for some reason or another never go after it. Is there a new job or degree that you'd love to have? Are you taking steps to get it?

Small steps are fine, just as long as you're moving forward.

so ca

Questions to think about...

- How often have you been stopped by reluctance to take action?

- Do you like to do research to determine what action you should take?

to journal: How easy is it for you to take small steps to reach your goals?

CLEARING

> *"I don't need time. What I need is a deadline."*
>
> –Duke Ellington

Is clutter taking over your life?

Okay, maybe it's not that dramatic, but clutter drains energy. It's a reminder of things left undone.

Each day take one step to clear away the mail, clothing, magazines or whatever needs to be put away. Make a commitment to clear away an item (or items) every day.

You'll find that when you clear the clutter you also free up your energy—and who couldn't use more of that?

Are you ready to get started? It can seem daunting to clear things away if they've been left to pile up over time. Follow the steps below so you can get things done with a minimum of stress.

1. Don't attempt to clear everything away at once. Give yourself time to get things done.

2. Set aside a time each week to sort through the clutter. Make an appointment with yourself and keep it!

3. Reward yourself when you've accomplished your weekly goal. Make sure you acknowledge your progress.

ᘄ ᘓ

Questions to think about…

- Do you reward yourself when you reach a goal?

- Where is the clutter in your life?

✐ *to journal:* **Why do you let things build up?**

MOVING THROUGH FEAR

> *"There are only two ways to live your life. One is as though nothing is a miracle. The other is as though everything is a miracle."*
>
> —Albert Einstein

The other day I got an email from a gentleman named, Tim. He asked me for advice about looking for a new job. He was unemployed and money was running low, but he wanted to make a fresh start.

How much courage does it take to transform your life after it's come undone? Having been through this situation myself more than once, I'd say it takes quite a lot. That's the difference between those people who survive and those who thrive. Survival is going from one crisis to the next, always shocked and a little surprised that you made it. Thriving is a totally different experience.

When you thrive you are not expecting doom at every turn. Your life isn't just an endless journey through anxiety and insecurity. Yes, things do happen and life is not always a big bowl of cherries. I'm not saying you'll never be hurt or disappointed; but I am saying that how you react to those things will determine your life experience. We can spend a lifetime blaming this one or that one, being a victim of circumstances and believing that someone else took our stuff. Lots of people do it everyday. If that appeals to you, I certainly won't discourage it. However, if you love your life no matter what—you are thriving. That's something no one can ever take away from you.

At the end of Tim's email, he admitted to being uneasy about the changes he was about to make. He acknowledged his fears, but then he said he wanted a better life and was going to take the steps to get it. From the outside his life may not look very attractive, but with that admission he's already made the move from surviving into thriving. I'm excited for him, and I'm looking forward to hearing about his progress.

How about you—are you ready to make the move? If so, here are some steps you can take.

1. Get clear of negative people and negative influences. If someone is always telling you what can't be done or how awful everything is, you won't benefit from being in that energy.

2. Take some quiet time everyday. Whether you call it meditating or being alone with your thoughts, take time for yourself.

3. Keep learning new things. Once you decide you know it all, you will never grow beyond that point.

4. Write down your ideas and your goals. There's something about writing them down that makes them real.

5. Laugh. Not only is laughing healthy, but it's much more attractive as well. Who would you rather be with—someone who laughs or someone who's always grumpy?

6. Love yourself, a lot.

7. Embrace life. Don't wait for some terrible event to occur before you appreciate what you have.

I've been in survival mode and in thriving mode, and I can tell you that thriving is much better. No, fear doesn't completely go away, but it stops being a way of life. We all have the power to go from surviving to thriving, and in the end it's up to us to make it happen.

೫ ೞ

Questions to think about…

- Do you feel that you are surviving or thriving?

- What negative influences (if any) are surrounding you?

✏ to journal: **Have you ever felt like a victim of circumstances?**

SUCCESS

"I couldn't wait for success, so I went ahead without it."

Jonathan Winters

Most people say that they want to move past limiting beliefs. What's the first step? Change your perspective. Make a decision. Take action. A lot of us have beliefs we're raised with, that we accept and never question. Start questioning. Give yourself permission to step out of the box. Challenge yourself.

You can have the success you want to achieve. No one else can create it for you. It's yours if you're ready to go beyond what you've always accepted to be true. Be willing to take a chance. Make the leap and claim what is yours.

∽ ∾

Questions to think about…

- How do you define success?

- What expectations are limiting you right now?

✎ *to journal:* **Have you ever been told that you can only go so far in life?**

CHAPTER 8: STAYING MOTIVATED

"You will do foolish things, but do them
with enthusiasm."

−Colette

Even if you have passion and drive to pursue your dreams, you will run out of steam eventually. Disappointments and setbacks will come up no matter how hard we work. Motivation and support will help to keep us going even when we're doubting ourselves or are just too tired to continue. Take care of yourself by getting proper rest and taking time to meditate and journal. It's important to reinforce yourself so you can keep going when things are rough. (You'll find a list of books and videos in the For More Information section that will help you to stay on track.)

PROCRASTINATION

"Each of us has that right, that possibility, to invent ourselves daily. If a person does not invent herself, she will be invented. So, to be bodacious enough to invent ourselves is wise."

—Maya Angelou

Is procrastination a challenge? Are you putting off doing something—like starting an exercise program or looking for a new job?

We may procrastinate because we're afraid of making a change or perhaps the task just seems to overwhelming for us to handle.

Unfortunately the more we procrastinate, the bigger the thing we're avoiding becomes. Write down the steps that are needed to take action, then prioritize. Break large steps into smaller ones and set realistic time lines.

Don't be hard on yourself. Creating stress only adds to your desire to keep putting things off!

Take it a step at a time. You may find things flowing much easier.

❧ ❧

Questions to think about…

- How often do you procrastinate?

- Do you find that it's hard to get started on projects?

✎ to journal: **How do you deal with stress in your life?**

FACING OBSTACLES

"Energy flows where attention goes."
–Dr. Michael Beckwith

A friend of mine was saying how hard it was to look for another job. Having gone through a few careers myself, one thing I've learned is that looking for a job is a job in itself.

It can be tiring and sometimes demoralizing to apply for jobs and never hear anything back. Or to go on interviews where people say they'll call and they don't. It can take a lot out of a person, and make them wonder if they really have anything to offer.

When you're out there job-hunting, frustration and fatigue can set in and giving up (if you can afford to) starts looking very attractive. What kept me going was staying focused on my end result. Getting over one hurdle made me stronger for the next one, and the next.

Think about it—are you facing obstacles or opportunities?

‿ ‿

Questions to think about…

• Have you ever gone after something and been discouraged when you had no result?

• What projects have you focused on and completed successfully?

to journal: **Do you see obstacles in front of you right now?**

YOU ARE ENOUGH

> *"Take a day to heal yourself of the lies you have been told about yourself and then, go out and heal someone else."*
>
> —Maya Angelou

It is possible that at some time in your life you got the message that you weren't enough. You weren't smart enough, attractive enough, rich enough...just not the "right" type of person to have what you desired in life.

It is possible that well-meaning people close to you gave you this message. Or you learned it out in the world.

The thing is, you are enough just as you are.

The world is waiting for what you have to share.

It's not about waiting for someone else to rescue us, or make things right. We can do that for ourselves right now.

Are you ready?

Take a step in a positive direction by surrounding yourself with people who uplift you, as opposed to the ones who bring you down.

Look for ways to keep a positive and optimistic mindset, instead of always thinking about what's wrong.

The more you believe in yourself, the more you can express your gifts and talents in the world.

∞ ○ℛ

Questions to think about…

- What do you feel are your special gifts?

- Are there people around you who give you praise and support?

✍ *to journal:* **What type of people do you feel are more likely to be successful?**

BELIEF

> *"Some people say, motivation doesn't last.*
> *Well neither does bathing. That's why*
> *I recommend doing both daily."*
>
> –Zig Ziglar

When you are motivated to get something done, you'll work hard to accomplish your task. The downside is that once that task has been completed, the motivation can begin to fade.

Just ask anyone who has gone on a diet and has ended up gaining the weight back. The initial excitement and motivation fades away little by little, and you're back into your old habits.

Motivation and belief in your end result has to be reinforced everyday.

∞ ∞

Questions to think about…

- What are you doing to motivate yourself to keep moving forward?

- Are you reading positive books and surrounding yourself with like-minded people?

to journal: **How are you staying motivated so you can reach your goals?**

FAILING FORWARD

"Your destiny is not your history!"
–Camellia M. Johnson

If people aren't making mistakes, they aren't learning. Instead, you get people who pretend to know what they don't know—which just creates more problems in the long run.

When you're afraid to fail...to stumble...to look silly...you will stay stuck in your comfort zone. Mastery is nice, but it's also darned boring.

You have to be willing to fail if you want to grow.

Failure is a tough thing in our society. Everyone loves a winner, the saying goes. But those winners had to fail, probably more than once, on their way to winning.

There are no overnight successes. There are just people who kept going when others gave up.

☙ ❧

Questions to think about…

• How do you feel when you think about failure?

• Have you ever achieved something that took you a long time to accomplish?

✎ to journal: **What lessons have you learned when you've failed at something?**

GRATITUDE

"The hardest arithmetic to master is that which enables us to count our blessings."

–Eric Hoffer

When the New Year comes it's expected that we'll think about the new things we want in our lives. We're supposed to make resolutions with lists of things we're going to start doing. Often it seems those resolutions don't last very long because we may not be ready to do the necessary work to make those changes happen.

I think along with focusing on what we want, we should also be thankful for what we have. If we're not grateful for what we have now, it'll be harder to get other things we want.

The catch is that if you appreciate what you have, it'll be easier to move on to what you want. I know that sounds contradictory.

Your experiences are adding to your knowledge. Whether you're learning patience from dealing with customers, or a demanding manager, or a promotion you didn't get. Everything you're experiencing is helping to propel you to the next level.

For me it became easier when I stopped being pissed off about not having what I wanted. I put myself in a place of being thankful for what I had (no matter how messed up I thought it was) and grateful for the opportunities I knew were coming.

❧ ❧

Questions to think about…

- What are you grateful for in your life?

- Have you looked back on your lessons learned?

to journal: **Do you focus on what you have or on what you wish you had?**

CONCLUSION

"Far away, there in the sunshine, are my highest aspirations...I can look up and see their beauty, believe in them, and try to follow where they lead."
–Louisa May Alcott

What you are most excited about will be what you put the most effort into—but it won't feel like effort. You have certain skills and abilities that come naturally. Identify them and play them up in your work and life. Contrary to what you may have been taught, life is not meant to be a struggle. When you connect with your passion you will also connect with your purpose.

Tips for Staying On Track

- See that bringing your vision into reality is a process and will take time.

- Allow yourself to make mistakes and have down days—pick yourself up again and keep going.

- Discomfort can be a sign that you are about to challenge yourself—and make the leap to a higher level. Accept it's natural when you are doing something new or unfamiliar.

- Trust your "gut" instincts—if it feels totally wrong for you, don't do it. If it's just "stage fright" then the discomfort will be temporary and will disappear once you get started.

- Be open and willing to learn.

- See opportunities in every situation.

- Write down your ideas.

QUESTIONS & ANSWERS

Here are some frequently asked questions I've received about what happens when you decide to make shifts in your thinking. You may want to create a vision and experience all of the good things that are waiting to materialize, but in the meantime it can be tough to go through the transition. Perhaps some of these questions and answers will apply to what you're feeling right now.

Q: It's nice to have a vision, but how do I discover what I'm supposed to be doing with my life?

A: That's something we've all asked ourselves at one time or another. I've certainly asked it often enough, which is what led me to make many changes in my career and my life.

How do you discover what you're supposed to be doing? First, understand that your purpose is whatever YOU say it is. You know it when you feel yourself drawn to certain types of things. What brings you joy? What makes you happy? What comes effortlessly for you? Is there something you do that people always ask your opinion about? Look there for your purpose.

You already know what you want to do, you just have to give yourself permission to start doing it.

Often the thing that we most want to do is the thing that we most fear doing. Perhaps we're afraid of being humiliated. Or we're afraid to fail—or afraid to succeed. So many of us have been conditioned to hide what we're good at so that we can fit in and not stand out.

Many people pursue celebrity because they feel getting attention will somehow feed their craving for connecting with their life purpose. But that emptiness inside will not be filled by attention, or by more money, more love...more stuff will not fill the longing we have deep inside of ourselves. It will only be filled when we love ourselves enough to say, I am going to be the very best I can be in the world. I am going to accept my joy and express the best part of myself.

Q: How can I stay focused on what I want to happen when everything in my life seems to be falling apart right now?

A: Unfortunately it can be a challenge to create a vision for what you desire while you're distracted by what isn't working in the present. If you're having issues with lack of money, a relationship breakup or a failing business you won't have a lot of energy to put into creating your desired life. The catch here is that the more you focus on what isn't working, the more you'll be frustrated by what isn't working.

Your frustration will block your creativity and make it next to impossible for you to hear (or trust) your inner guidance. Instead you'll make decisions out of fear and desperation and those decisions will just bring you more of what you don't want. Or you may be stuck and unable to make a decision because first you want validation that your action will be the "right" one. Either way you won't be in a position to visualize the things that you desire. You certainly won't be able to stay focused on them because your energy will be depleted by worry and anxiety.

Creating and staying focused on your vision will require a huge amount of belief and trust. Even if you don't see any outside evidence, you will have to stay on track with your desires. Start out by writing down your vision and creating a vision board or mind map if possible. You'll need to be able to reinforce your vision, so having something you can refer to will make it easier. There will be occasions when you will have doubts. Having visual reminders of what your life will look like once your vision is created will make it easier for you to stay focused. Just remember that you don't have to be perfect when you're doing this. The most important thing is to take the step forward, no matter how small it is.

Q: How do I find work that I'm passionate about?

A: What makes you excited? What do you enjoy? In order to find passionate work you have to find out what you are passionate about. This is why starting with a vision can help you. When you create this vision and just let it flow without judging what comes to mind, you'll uncover things that you really want to have. Don't worry so much about finding the passion, let the feeling lead you to your meaningful work.

Q: **How can I keep my spirits up and stay hopeful while I'm making changes in my life?**

A: That's the tough one, isn't it? This is where regular connection to your vision will help you to maintain your enthusiasm. You can also use this time to listen to your inner guidance so that you can take actions that will move you forward. You have to make the effort to stay on track. It won't happen on its own. (This is also where the motivational "tips" in this book will come in very handy!)

Q: **How do I move into taking action?**

A: Consider what is the step that makes the most sense to you? How do you feel about it? If you feel bad, then that's your intuition warning you that this may not be the right thing to do at this time. Remember action may be one small step. Don't feel that you have to only take big leaps in order to take action. If you have to break it down into small steps, do so. Once you take that step it will be easier to take the next one.

℘ ℞

ACKNOWLEDGEMENTS

A big thank you to author, Kelli Wilkins who was a tremendous help with editing, feedback, and suggestions.

Thanks to Julie Barnes for her feedback as I was writing this book and her assistance on my other projects.

Thank you to Annemarie Segaric for her coaching and support while I started my own journey into entrepreneurship.

FOR MORE INFORMATION

For more information about the topics in this book, please visit my website http://www.dbaileycoach.com for articles and resources and information about mentoring, group workshops and products to support your transformation.

Here are a list of books and movies that I've used to support my own personal development. Of course, it's even better if you're being entertained while you're learning! Look for them at your local library or purchase them to add them to your personal library. If I'm feeling down or need reinforcement, I find myself turning to my favorite books and videos to pick me up again.

Books

Release Your Brilliance: The 4 Steps to Transforming Your Life and Revealing Your Genius to the World by Simon T. Bailey (Harper Business, 2007).

Life Visioning: A Four-Stage Evolutionary Journey to Live as Divine Love by Michael Bernard Beckwith (Agape Media International, 2008).

Think Big: Unleashing Your Potential for Excellence by Ben Carson with Cecil Murphey (Zondervan, 1992).

The Alchemist by Paulo Coelho (HarperCollins, 1993).

Excuses Begone! by Wayne W Dyer (Hay House Inc., 2009).

The Dark Side of the Light Chasers: Reclaiming Your Power, Creativity, Brilliance and Dreams by Debbie Ford (Riverhead Books, 1998).

Excuse Me, Your Life is Waiting: The Astonishing Power of Feelings by Lynn Grabhorn (Hampton Roads Publishing, 2003).

You Can Heal Your Life by Louise L. Hay (Hay House, Inc., 1999).

What You Say When You Talk to Yourself by Shad Helmstetter (Pocket, 1990).

Ask and It Is Given: Learning to Manifest Your Desires by Esther & Jerry Hicks (Hay House, Inc., 2004).

Left to Tell: Discovering God Amidst the Rwandan Holocaust by Immaculee Ilibagiza, (Hay House, Inc., 2006).

What's Possible! 50 True Stories of People Who Dared To Dream They Could Make a Difference by Daryn Kagan (Meredith Books, 2008).

The War of Art: Break Through the Blocks and Win Your Inner Creative Battles by Steven Pressfield (Grand Central Publishing, 2002).

Step Into the Right Career: 107 Tips to Change Your Life While Still Paying the Bills by Annemarie Segaric (Segaric Coaching, Inc., 2008).

The Power of Now: A Guide to Spiritual Enlightenment by Eckhart Tolle (New World Library, 2004).

The Soul of Money: Reclaiming the Wealth of Our Inner Resources by Lynne Twist (W.W. Norton & Company, 2003).

The Value in the Valley: A Black Woman's Guide Through Life's Dilemmas by Iyanla Vanzant (Simon & Schuster, 1995).

Movies

Finding Forrester. G. Van Sant, Director (Columbia Pictures, 2001).

Muriel's Wedding. P.J. Hogan, Director (Miramax, 1995).

Pleasantville. G. Ross, Director (New Line Cinema, 2004)

The Count of Monte Cristo. K. Reynolds, Director (Touchstone Pictures, 2002).

The Secret. D. Heriot, Director (Prime Time Productions, 2006).

The Secret Life of Bees. G. Prince-Bythewood, Director (20th Century Fox, 2008).

The Shawshank Redemption. F. Darabont, Director (Castle Rock Entertainment, 2004).

Wall-e. A. Stanton, Director (Walt Disney Studios, 2008).

What the Bleep Do We Know? B. Chasse, M. Vicente, W. Arntz, Directors (20th Century Fox, 2005).

You Can Heal Your Life: The Movie. M. Goorjian, Director (Hay House, Inc., 2007).

ABOUT THE AUTHOR

Deborah A. Bailey is a sought after expert to discuss today's most pressing business and career transition issues. Deborah helps clients to shift their thinking and make the transition from employee to entrepreneur.

After earning her B.A. degree in English from Douglass College, she went into a career in fashion and retail, earning an A.A.S. in Advertising and Communications from the Fashion Institute of Technology. She made career transitions from fashion copywriting to working at companies such as AT&T, Lucent Technologies and Johnson & Johnson.

After several years in the corporate world, Deborah graduated from Coach U and successfully transitioned to career consultant and coach by founding her company, Deb Bailey Coaching. Her extensive experience in the employee to entrepreneur transition, and employee coaching have made her the partner of choice for many successful entrepreneurs and career professionals.

Deborah is the host of "Women Entrepreneurs—The Secrets of Success," a weekly internet radio talk show. Deborah provides candid discussions with today's top entrepreneurs, authors and industry experts such as former CNN anchor Daryn Kagan and inventor and QVC personality, Lori Greiner.

A published author, Deborah has had bylines in Baseline magazine, Dailyworth. com, Identity magazine, Bankrate.com, Working World, The Bridges, Daily Career Connection, More.com and Women&Biz.com and posted as the Career Changer blogger on the Women for Hire network. She's been a guest on TV and various radio stations, including WSVA 550AM, WJON, WBT, WEPM, WLW 700 Cincinnati, the Stu Taylor Show, 710 KURV, the NJ Perspectives show on ABC6 TV and Fox News Strategy Room as an expert in career transitions and reinvention. Deborah has been quoted in The Wall Street Journal, Crain's NY Business, Golf Course Industry, InStore magazine, Moneywatch and Glass Hammer magazine.

Deborah is founder of DBC Communications, a communications company which produces internet radio shows, e-books, audios and workshops.

Made in the USA
Lexington, KY
04 May 2012